Jumping is Jumping

JANE WALLACE

Jumping is Jumping

How to Achieve Success Over Any Fence

Photographs by Kit Houghton

Methuen London

First published in Great Britain 1994
by Methuen London
an imprint of Reed Consumer Books Ltd
Michelin House, 81 Fulham Road, London SW3 6RB
and Auckland, Melbourne, Singapore and Toronto

A CIP catalogue record for this book is
available from the British Library
ISBN 0 413 67360 X

Phototypeset by Deltatype Ltd,
Ellesmere Port, Cheshire

Printed in Hong Kong
by Mandarin Offset Ltd

To all my pupils, who over the
years have made me scratch
my head in deciding the
best method of explanation
for jumping correctly, and
from whom I derive great
pleasure (most of the time!)

Contents

Foreword

I have been lucky enough to know Jane Wallace both as a friend and as a competitor for over ten years. During those times when we were both competing at the highest levels of the sport, Jane was always one of the more stylish and classical riders around the Horse Trials. As such, her greatest successes – when winning Burghley on King's Jester in 1988 and the silver medal in the European Championships in 1989 – were richly deserved.

Being such a stylish rider, Jane understood more than most, even while she was competing, the importance of the classical principles of jumping. These principles were meticulously developed in the cavalry schools of Italy, France, Sweden, America and at Weedon in England. That style of riding is still very much taught in Italy, France and America today, and most of the rest of the world, and the Germans in particular, are increasingly imitating the classical style.

As classical riding prevails more and more, be it from Europe, the Americas or the Antipodes, I always find it curious that we in Great Britain tend to be reluctant to follow the trend. Jane Wallace was an exception to that rule as a competitor and now as an instructor and trainer she stands out as a disciple of the classical school.

Today, her depth of understanding is much greater even than when she was competing. When reading *Jumping is Jumping*, I keep hearing the words of some of the greatest horsemen and trainers in the world. All say things a little differently while still after the same goal. Jane preaches the gospel in her words – words which she has found her pupils best relate to.

Both pictorially and literally, *Jumping is Jumping* is very worthwhile reading for all who teach or jump fences of whatever type. For those who aspire, I would strongly recommend that they study this book with great care.

Captain Mark Phillips

Preface

I hope that this book will give heart to all those who think they have left it too late to succeed. I started eventing seriously when I was 30 years old and wore a Union Jack on my jacket four years later.

I attribute my ability to event successfully at top level to all the hunting and dressage I did as a child and to the show-jumping and point-to-pointing I did in my twenties, for the same principles apply to jumping any fence correctly, whatever the pace.

Acknowledgements

I should like to thank Kit Houghton for searching through his thousands of photographs to find suitable pictures to illustrate each point and Mark Phillips for writing the Foreword and, along with Jimmy Wofford, for giving me inspiration and food for thought.

I am also grateful to David Broome for permission to quote him and to Katie Wilkinson for posing for Figure 26 – this is not what she normally looks like!

Note on Illustrations

A variety of photographs has been chosen to illustrate this book. My comments on them stem from what is shown in the photograph, with no pre-conceived ideas or assumptions about what might have happened before or afterwards in some of the action pictures.

Although the camera never lies, it can be misleading and can show odd angles which give a false impression. The pictures I have chosen are ones which I feel illustrate best the particular points I am trying to explain. I hope that none of the comments I have made will cause offence – it is easy to be critical when sitting in a chair. Having ridden at a high level myself, I do feel that I am in a position to make the occasional 'critical appraisal', but far be it from me to criticise anyone unduly! With any luck, some of the things I have said might prove useful or helpful for the future.

It is no coincidence that it was easier to find 'good' examples from the best riders. Good balance means good position – a lack of balance or security of seat will provide a moderate photograph. With the odd exception, there are few good, effective riders who have poor positions. American riders are often criticised for just having 'pretty' positions and for lacking effectiveness. However, effective riding is far easier to learn from a correct basic position than from a bad one.

On arriving somewhere in the approximate area of take-off, I let the horse take command and jump the fence. I try to be an uninterfering passenger from there to the other side, and then I take up command again.

David Broome

Introduction

When browsing along the equestrian shelves of any bookshop, one is faced with a mesmerising number of books on jumping: show-jumping, cross-country, grid-work, training the show-jumper, training the event horse – the list is endless. There are few, if any, books, however, which cover the *whole* subject of jumping, encompassing not only show-jumping and cross-country but steeplechase and the mental approach to it all.

The aim of this book is to explain that, although each discipline varies in the pace required, all forms of jumping boil down to the same basics. Indeed, the foundation of all correct work both on the flat and over fences is the thorough and established work done at the lowest level of training. Provided that the horse is going forward, straight, balanced and in a rhythm, with the necessary impulsion, he will be able to perform whatever is required of him. The pace of the approach and the complexity of the fence are therefore immaterial. This is why this book is called *Jumping is Jumping*, for the same formulae apply to whatever type of fence at whatever speed it is being negotiated.

The idea for this book came when it was suggested to me that my rise to wearing a Union Jack on my jacket to represent Great Britain in three-day eventing after only four years could be termed meteoric. I was then forced to explain that although, due to lack of opportunity, I did not start eventing seriously until I was 30 years old, I had well and truly served my apprenticeship during the preceding years.

I was fortunate, in 1982, to be given the ride on John and Maryan Huntridge's horse, Marsh Heron. Heron was out of Novice but had yet to compete at Intermediate level. By the end of the year he was well into Advanced and had won Windsor and been well placed at Osberton three-day events. The following year Heron was sidelined to a great extent by injury, but still finished 3rd in the Open Championships at Locko Park. He was a horse plagued by injury of one sort or another, so we did not get our chance to have our first run at Badminton until two years later, when we finished 8th in 1986 – the year of the mud. King's Jester, in the same ownership, was Advanced by this stage as a seven-year-old. Jester came to me as a five-year-old with a reputation of having a very difficult character – no exaggeration! – but it was he who allowed me to realise my dream of representing my country officially in 1986 at Bialy Bor in Poland and he and I went on to be in the British squad twice more, be short-listed for the Olympic Games, win Bramham CCI on two consecutive occasions, win Burghley CCI and win a European silver medal.

In 1990, after eight years of concentrated eventing, I felt that I had realised all my ambitions, and, having suffered from back problems for many years, I decided to retire 'at the top' and turn my attention to training young horses and pupils.

I attribute this quick rise to success in eventing to the years of 'preparatory' work I had done since I was a child. My balance was learnt by riding ponies bareback from Midsummer Common in Cambridge to Cherry Hinton Riding School, a famous local establishment run by the tireless, enthusiastic inspiration to all Pony Clubbers and would-be competitors, Liz Pickard. From the age of six or seven I would work for my rides and this continued for many years, so I had the advantage of riding a myriad different horses and ponies.

Riding Davina Whiteman's top-class show ponies for nine years may not have taught me anything about jumping, but it did teach me how to stay relaxed on an oated-up pony when under pressure at a top show in front of hundreds of people. It also taught me ring-craft – vital too in the dressage arena – and how to present an animal to the best without showing what you were doing. All this became invaluable when riding in front of crowds at events when nerves were on high tension. I learnt how to control my nerves and how to hide them completely from my horse.

From my showing days, I progressed to a hunter livery yard where I 'messed around' on horses, with hunting, schooling, the occasional one-day event (never very successful), and then point-to-pointing. I was working a six-day week, and on my day off I would rise even earlier to go to ride out for Willie Stephenson at Royston. I loved it. There, I learnt how to gallop a horse, how to settle one and how to find my balance riding short. This was the beginning of my final education. Racing teaches all that is natural about horse and rider – there is no time for niceties. It is a case of 'getting on with it' yet always maintaining the basics of rhythm and balance.

Coupled with this knowledge gained from riding racehorses, I was moving on to producing young horses for show-jumping.

The final pieces of the jigsaw were beginning to fall into place and I was slowly starting fully to understand *how* a horse jumped and what was the best way for a rider to help his horse to jump correctly.

By riding so many different horses, learning how to show-jump and how to ride fast work and jump fences at speed, my education was what could be termed 'rounded'. Of course, you never stop learning, and horses are the greatest teachers of all, but I had a thorough grounding by the time I turned my hand to eventing full time. As a result, I found success immediately with a talented horse.

During these formative years, I had few lessons but studied hard by watching riders and horses I admired and then experimenting with the horses I was riding at the time. Every discipline has its masters. John Francome was a delight and an inspiration to watch. His success underlines my theories in that he was a highly successful show-jumper before he turned to racing. He applied the same principles to each and, coupled with his ability to balance a horse and his excellent eye for a stride, this put him in a different class from his fellow jockeys. I would study how John rode with avid interest and I would think hard on how he cajoled even the most ignorant horse into jumping well.

The late Caroline Bradley was one of my inspirations in show-jumping. Her classical and quiet way of riding, and her ability to encourage horses to spring over their fences as if they had taken off on springboards, was fascinating to watch. I would study what she did and then try to emulate it on my horses at home. By copying her methods, I suddenly found that I, too, could make horses jump much higher and be quicker off the ground when taking off. This ability to teach horses *how* to jump was never taught to me. I learnt how to do it merely by watching and studying. I am a great believer in the fact that although you can be taught many things, it is you, yourself, who can learn the most. Do not wait or expect to be taught. Learn for yourself. So much is there for us to see and study and so learn accordingly. Learn what is right and what is wrong. When a horse refuses or knocks down a fence, ask yourself why. Then put that answer into practice when you ride and jump a fence. Of course, some people are more naturally talented as riders than others, but we can all learn by example, provided that we make the effort and possess a sufficiently inquiring mind. It is only when you truly understand how a horse physically lifts itself into the air with a rider on its back that you will be able consistently to achieve good results.

The event world provides us with a mixture of talents. Some riders excel at one sphere more than another, but the truly great rider excels at all. Mark Todd is the example of a brilliant all-round horseman. Not only has he won two Olympic three-day event gold medals, but he also wins at top level in show-jumping and has ridden successfully in steeplechases. Again, as with John Francome, he provides an example of someone who puts the same theory into practice.

The slightly depressing side of horse sports is that you are only ever as good as the horse you are riding. However, a well-trained horse with limited talent will be superior to one with an enormous amount of ability who has been poorly educated. So this is the challenge. Producing an ordinary horse to perform immaculately so that he becomes a very good horse is immensely satisfying. Anyone can ride a good horse, but it takes dedication and skill to train a less talented horse to the same high level. In order to achieve this, the rider and trainer must have a deep-rooted understanding of how to produce the most from a horse. The purpose of this book is to try to explain how to achieve the best result when jumping all types of fences and how to train a horse to cope with the different disciplines required for each.

In my book *The Less-Than-Perfect Horse*, I cover in detail the stages of training which, when established correctly, produce a well-educated horse. The initial schooling steps are the same for whatever activity the horse is destined but variations will occur as the training progresses to higher and more specific levels. The basics must be correct and sound for the continuation to advanced levels to run without problems. These later problems are most commonly due to some fault which has passed unnoticed or been ignored at an earlier stage of training. Jumping will emphasise any problem which is evident on the flat, so this basic flat work is of paramount importance. *The Less-Than-Perfect Horse* also covers jumping problems and is a useful companion to this book.

In this book I have covered the type of horse suitable for the various disciplines and the technique of jumping necessary for success. I also discuss warming-up procedure for both cross-country and show-jumping, because this is influential in producing clear rounds, and course-walking because, again, careful walking of the course often makes the difference between faults and clear rounds. In a three-day event, the roads and tracks play a large part so these too are covered, as is the speed for cross-country. Different types of cross-country fence are discussed and how to tackle them to avoid problems, and the steeplechase phase is explained in detail.

The object of the book is to help a rider to complete a three-day event, as the ultimate goal, without jumping penalties and with as few time penalties as possible. By teaching your horse how to jump correctly, it means that you can aim to jump the most difficult and direct route wherever practicable and so save time. This means that a non-thoroughbred horse has a good chance of doing a fast time cross-country even if he is not the speediest (for example, Ginny Elliot's Priceless). A well-trained horse which stops and turns on demand will be quicker over the course than a faster but less disciplined horse which takes a long time to pull up and will not turn accurately.

As well as the *horse* being well-trained and disciplined, the rider must also work on himself or herself to gain maximum efficiency. A weak, unbalanced rider with an insecure position will be of no assistance to even the best-schooled horse. Security of seat and leg are of paramount importance and will be discussed in the first chapter.

I hope that this book will also give heart to all those people who think that they have left it too late to succeed. Provided that you have served your apprenticeship to the horse by studying and practising the various riding disciplines, there is no reason why you cannot succeed as I did. Had I, myself, been 'sound', there is no reason why I could not have started even later or still be riding at top level. You only have to look at the ages of our top event riders to realise that experience counts enormously. Competition experience is vital. It is only when under the stress of competing that reactions are tested to the full. Jumping calls for split-second reactions which are never tested at home to the same extent. So do not despair if the chance to event has not yet come your way. Make the most of your time by competing in as many show-jumping and cross-country competitions as you can and jump as often as possible.

One word of warning, however: confidence is all-important when jumping, so do try to avoid losing your confidence by riding 'bad' horses. 'Bad' horses are those unfortunate animals which lack good basic training and as a result are so ignorant that they do not know how to jump, falling or refusing on an all-too-regular basis. They themselves lose confidence and certainly cause the rider to ride incorrectly and with little faith. These horses have a detrimental effect on the way a rider tackles his fences and there are many riders who, as a result of always riding moderate horses, have lost the ability to ride a good horse. So, gain experience on as many horses as possible, but try to avoid riding horses which have irreparably lost their confidence or whose attitude will eventually make you lose yours.

My attitude over the years when riding moderate horses is to stick to what I know is the correct way of riding and training and to avoid falling into the traps of short-cuts, gadgets or even brute force which are unfortunately sometimes the only ways to 'improve' or succeed with some animals. I have found that horses which find basic work impossible invariably have something physically wrong with them. Whereas some physical problems can be improved with training, others are merely exacerbated, and it is this type of horse with which I cannot cope myself as a rider. I like to know that the horse is capable of doing what I ask of him, otherwise I find it unfair on him and soul-destroying for me. (Fortunately, everyone is different, because if we all had my attitude there would be many horses without riders!)

Understanding a horse's problems and preserving his confidence during training is imperative, especially when it comes to jumping. Knowing when and what to ask a horse to jump only comes with experience; experience which can be gained from time spent with all sorts of horses, by watching and noticing when other people have problems. By watching carefully when you are side-lined without a ride, you can learn so much. This can then be put into practice when it is your turn. Do not be negative when you are horseless – you can use the time to great advantage. I did, and it all paid off in the end, however hard it may have seemed at the time.

Chapter 1

Horses and Riders

Type and conformation

In the same way that a Morris Minor, for example, is not suitable for motor racing, so some types of horse are not suitable for jumping. For a horse to be able to jump well, he must be an athlete. He must also have power, courage and be correct enough in his conformation not to suffer physically with strains or other disabling problems. A show-jumper must combine power and scope of jump with being careful, athletic and courageous. He must have sufficient quality to enable him to gallop against the clock. Speed and stamina are not as vital in the show-jumper as in the event horse, who must also have courage, scope and athleticism.

Most of the factors which make up a good jumper can be seen in the horse's conformation and movement. What are not always obvious, however, are the horse's mental aptitude and potential courage. Courage and bravery are closely associated with the horse's training. Careless and hurried training can easily wreck a horse's confidence, whereas patient and thorough training will give him time to learn and develop so that he can respond without question or doubt when asked to jump difficult fences. A horse which finds jumping easy and within his range will invariably be bolder than a horse which struggles to clear a fence. Picture in your mind a horse which jumps very boldly, be it a show-jumper, event horse or racehorse. By the very nature of its bold jump, the horse is displaying its scope and power. It is therefore easy for him to give extravagant leaps.

All these factors must be borne in mind when choosing a horse for jumping. Not only must you decide on what sphere you wish to concentrate, but also at what level you would ideally like to train and achieve. There is no point in rushing out and buying an Olympic-type horse if all you want is to compete at Riding Club level. It is often the case that the most talented horse is temperamentally the most difficult, whereas the 'average' horse with limited ability is easy-going and uncomplicated. For the novice rider, this type of horse is a must. Trying to cope with a complex and difficult horse is taxing and can often take the fun out of jumping and competing. Be satisfied with an ordinary horse until you have gained sufficient experience to move on. After all, a learner driver, or someone having newly passed their driving test, is not given a Porsche to drive.

There never was a more appropriate saying when discussing horses' ability than ''Andsome is what 'andsome does'. A pretty, precious-looking horse often lives up to its looks and is a bit soft and namby-pamby. The more down-to-earth looking animal with an 'old-fashioned' head and workmanlike body will invariably be more robust and uncomplicated. Conformation is discussed in detail in *The Less-Than-Perfect Horse*, and I recommend the chapter in M. Horace Hayes's *Veterinary Notes for Horse Owners* on the relationship of soundness and conformation in the horse, but I will touch here on some of the more important aspects which concern jumping.

Conformation defects can affect a horse's performance, so it is important that he is well enough put together to be able to perform. For jumping a horse must have a good 'engine', i.e. powerful hindquarters with strength in his hocks. He must be able to bring his hocks well under him so that he can balance himself as well as propel and carry. This ability to use the hocks correctly is vital to a horse's performance. If he cannot bring his

1. Milton – winner of over £1,000,000 in prize money and arguably one of the greatest show-jumpers of all time. Note the power of the hindquarters and the length from hip to hock. He has a good shoulder and prominent wither and his head and neck are well put on. He is a beautifully balanced horse and is totally in proportion.

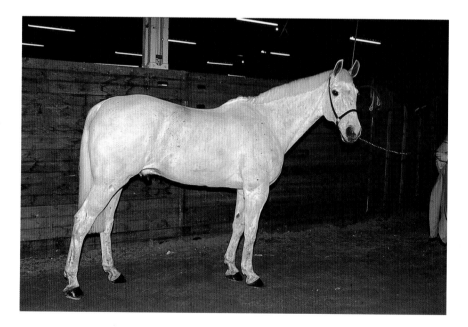

hocks underneath him, he will lack balance and self-carriage. A slightly bent hock gives greater leverage than a straight one but may err on the 'curby' side. Both King William and Master Craftsman, first and second at Badminton in 1992, have 'curby' hocks, which does not appear to affect their performance. In the show ring, however, this defect would put them near the bottom of the line.

Width between the hips gives power, as does length from the point of the hip to the hocks – well let down hocks is another term for this. Cow hocks are a sign of weakness and seldom found in a good jumper.

The most important factor when viewing a horse is to decide whether he is suitable for the job. He must have quality if he is to be a successful event horse but need not be full thoroughbred. He need not be 'beautiful' but he should have presence. He should strike you as being an athlete and bright and alert without being nervous or tense. Movement is all-important, and the horse should move with activity and good shoulder action, and, ideally, straight (although this is not a critical factor for powerful jumping). For a horse to be able to lift his shoulder and bend his knees over a fence, it is important that he moves in a way that enables him to jump well. A horse which 'daisy cuts' – in other words, floats along with hardly any bend to his knee – will find it difficult suddenly to lift and bend his knees over a fence. A little knee action in trot and particularly in canter generally indicates that the horse will find no difficulty in bending his knee over a fence. Too much knee action prevents the horse from galloping and lengthening and gives a choppy ride.

Size is a matter of personal choice, but I agree with the saying, 'If he's good enough, he's big enough.' As long as you feel comfortable and not under-horsed and you feel that you have plenty of power underneath you, you need not worry that your horse is too small. The bigger the horse, the more there is to go wrong with him – remember that Mark Todd's Charisma was under 16 hands and he was ridden to Olympic gold medal success by one of the tallest riders.

Whether to opt for a mare or a gelding is a matter of personal choice. Some people will not touch a mare, disliking the 'mareish' behaviour in evidence when she comes into season. Others swear by mares, vowing that they are far bolder and more honest than geldings. Mares *can* be a nuisance when they are in season, and it can prove a problem if mares and geldings are kept together. It may be difficult to turn them out with each other and

2. Charisma – dual Olympic Gold medal winner, ridden by Mark Todd. A power-packed little horse. Note the strength of hindquarters and the length from hip to hock. Perfectly in proportion, with a good shoulder and well-set-on head and neck, he won his second gold medal at the age of 16, which indicates how sound and tough he was. His conformation is difficult to fault – remember: conformation = soundness = performance.

3. Get Smart – represented Great Britain on no fewer than five consecutive occasions, completing Badminton to date without cross-country jumping penalties six times. A well-proportioned horse with a lovely shoulder, he shows a good example of a goose rump. He is standing naturally with his hocks well under him, but he does not show the same bend in the hock as Charisma or Milton, having a rather straighter hind leg. A real 'leg at each corner' horse. A sound, tough, well-balanced horse, indicating that his conformation means he does not put excessive strain on any one point. Note the difference in condition here between a fit horse and Charisma, who is well let down!

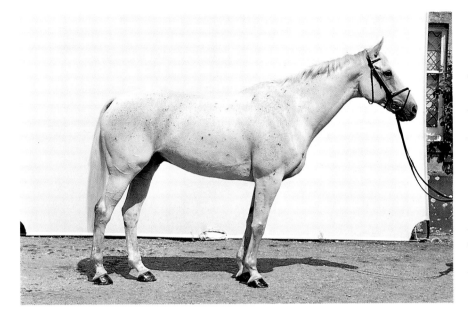

4. Glenburnie – winner of the European Championships in 1991. Not such a well-proportioned horse as Get Smart. He has a big front and great depth (which would indicate good stamina) but his hindquarters do not match his front and he has a straight hind leg, which would make it more difficult for him to find natural balance.

the mixture of the sexes provokes jealousy and fighting in many cases. A mare can be just as good as a gelding, but so often mares are not given the chance to prove themselves. I can think of as many moderate geldings as 'mareish' mares. It seems to be that the more successful mares are the more masculine types but this will only become apparent as the mare is put into work.

Jumping technique

Having decided that the horse you have seen standing still, in walk, trot and canter is suitable, the time has come for you to see him jump. The first jump is an important one to watch because it is then that the horse may indicate his true character. In the case of a young horse, he may balloon over the first couple of fences and then, because he gets tired so quickly, may just flop over the rest of the fences. When he is stronger and trained further, he will be able to reproduce his early leaps every time. If the early jumps are not seen, the impression will be of a horse jumping with little spring. An older horse may spook over the first fence, or creep over if he lacks boldness, which may point to lack of confidence or fear. When studying the actual jump of a horse, you should take note of the technique – that is, how he lifts his shoulders and hindquarters and how he lifts and bends his knees and hocks. A horse which drops his shoulder over every fence should be avoided.

11

You can forgive the occasional mistake in a young horse, but if he consistently drops his knees, or lets one leg hang down, he is more difficult to train successfully as a jumper. Of course all defects can be lessened with training, but there is little point in buying a horse for jumping whose natural style is poor. A horse will tend to revert to his natural way in moments of crisis, which is the very moment when you need perfect technique to get you

5. Delta and King's Jester – two successful horses with less-than-perfect foreleg techniques in these photos. The horse has dropped its shoulder in each case, causing the forearm to drop down and the lower foreleg to dangle. A horse must lift his shoulder (compare these photos with Figure 8b). Poor foreleg technique will catch out a horse in tricky moments, particularly when he is young and less experienced (as I found to my cost when I produced King's Jester as a novice!).

out of trouble. You should aim for a horse which lifts his shoulders and knees, keeping his toes up and level in front. Behind, he should lift his hindquarters and 'throw away' his hind legs, lifting his hocks and keeping his hind toes level. He should jump in an athletic manner – quick off the ground and quick to fold his forelegs. He should stretch his head and neck and round his back over the fence, making a good bascule.

6. A show-jumper with excellent foreleg technique: Livius with Peter Luther from Germany. Note how high the horse's knees are and how both these and the fetlocks and toes are level. (Compare this with the horses in Figure 5.)

7. Compare Jued Lad and Mark Todd here with Figure 5. The horse's knees are not 100 per cent level, but are still neat and tidy. (Note also the perfect position of the rider.)

8. Jumping a spread. An interesting sequence of pictures showing a horse in its three stages of jump: take-off, mid-air and landing. Note the free outline and total lack of restriction allowed to the horse by the rider. See how the hind legs have come together as the horse backs off, brings his hocks underneath him and lightens his forehand for take-off. The weight is obviously on the horse's hocks and not on his forehand (compare the horse's outline with that of a horse who is refusing). The rider is well in balance, with the upper body inclined forward – there is no need for him to be in behind his horse at a straightforward fence such as this. It is quite a big fence and the horse is experienced and trained to jump it. The horse's front leg technique is excellent and he is throwing a correct bascule (note the closeness of take-off point to the fence). The rider has allowed his weight to come out of his heel and the upper body is therefore collapsed over the horse's neck. The horse has 'thrown away' his hind legs and, although the rider has brought back his body in readiness for landing, there is no weight on the saddle, so allowing the horse freedom of his back throughout the jump. Notice how the horse brings his head up on landing to help his balance. If he should bring it too far up, he will cramp his hindquarters and be likely to hit the fence behind. This is a lovely sequence of a horse jumping well.

9. Excellent show-jumping hind leg technique. Milton's hind leg technique is brilliant, and you can see how he is clearing the spread fence with feet to spare by 'throwing away' his back end.

10. Note how when jumping from speed (or when jumping a drop fence) the hind legs are thrown out behind the horse rather than up and higher. Imagine what would happen if the horse had tried to clear the brush with his hind legs . . . and then if there were a drop. He could not keep his balance. Note how the rider has her weight back and seat low to keep balance and prevent the horse from going too high behind. Note also that her head is up and lower leg secure.

If a horse is incapable of rounding his back over a fence, his athletic ability will be adversely affected. It is only by having the ability to arch himself that the horse has full use of himself physically and all combination fences and trickily sited obstacles demand agile and athletic jumping from the horse. A hollow back indicates stiffness which will invariably cause problems somewhere along the line when jumping. What has to be decided when assessing a horse which jumps with a hollow back is whether the horse jumps in this way due to rider interference or whether he is genuinely stiff and rigid. If you settle on the former, you then must wonder whether the horse will be able to change his style of jumping or whether he has jumped so long in this way that it is well ingrained and unlikely to alter. Sometimes a horse is only able to lift his shoulders and knees when he jumps hollow and the moment he rounds his back he allows his shoulders and knees to drop down. A 'clever' rider can hide a multitude of sins, so beware!

The general impression should be of an elastic, athletic jump with scope and power. A young horse, being unbalanced, will often be misleading when jumping in his early days. He is often rather clumsy and uncoordinated and only gains speed of reaction as he becomes stronger and better balanced. This type of horse takes longer to train and requires time and patience to produce his best. A sharper horse is invariably quick on his feet from the very start, but may also be more difficult and complicated to train.

Young horses are often shown off jumping loose or on the lunge. This can be misleading because some horses jump well without a rider but cannot reproduce the same jump when ridden. I have found that the best horses are those which are naturally quick on their feet and if they hit a fence once are keen to avoid hitting it again. Some horses are natural jumpers and others take quite some time for the penny to drop on how they must gather themselves to leap into the air. In the same way as some people are naturally athletic, so some horses find jumping easier than others. Jumping well is tied in totally with how the horse is working on the flat, so the greener the horse, the more likely it is that his jumping will be hit-and-miss. If this is the case, look at how the horse jumps when he meets the fence on a good stride and note too how he copes when he meets it wrong. Ask yourself: has he the scope to make a big jump if necessary? Does he dangle his front legs straight down in moments of panic?

Of course it is difficult to make the correct decision when

choosing a horse, whether it is young or old. An older horse may have been badly ridden. He may have developed stiffnesses and resistances which affect his jump. You have to decide whether these can be improved or whether the horse jumps naturally in a particular way. It takes a long time for a horse to forget and a way of jumping might be so established that he may find it impossible to change.

Horses' conformation can be examined *ad infinitum* but unless there are some glaring faults, probably the most critical aspect of a horse is his temperament. A horse may be restricted in his physical ability but if he is willing to try his hardest then he will always be superior to a more talented horse which is reluctant to give his all. Temperament plays an enormous part in a successful horse, particularly the competition horse, although even for a hunter or a pleasant hack it is important. Temperament can be linked to training in that a well-trained, disciplined horse can learn to cope with a potentially neurotic and excitable temperament. An uneducated horse, like an uneducated child or dog, can be unpleasant to deal with. In the same way as a well-brought-up child is a delight, so a well-trained horse is a pleasure to ride and handle. However, some horses have an underlying streak of ungenerosity which makes them unwilling to try and therefore unrewarding to train. You cannot force a horse to jump, so if he really does not want to or is genuinely afraid, there is little that can be done to make him. There is scant pleasure to be had, in any case, in feeling that the horse is being made to do something which he hates doing. It is, on the other hand, a joy to ride a horse which you feel is enjoying his work. This willingness to work is to be encouraged from the early stages of training. If a horse should lose his faith in people, it is difficult to regain his confidence to the full. It is always a gamble, therefore, to buy a horse which is badly demoralised. It is ideal to produce your own young horse or, if you do not have sufficient experience, to acquire one from someone who has done a good job. A badly produced young horse, mismanaged and misunderstood, will be a problem to sort out. It requires experience and talent to produce one well, so make sure you realise the implications before committing yourself to a real youngster. If you do decide to buy a very green horse, do seek professional assistance by sending the horse for schooling and the pair of you having lessons. Avoid problems before they arrive – it makes life much easier.

To train a horse to jump takes time, effort and money. It is a waste of all these if the horse is not capable of doing what is required of him. There is nothing more depressing than trying your hardest to train something which is incapable of improving, so try to find a suitable animal as raw material so that you have a reward for all your efforts.

Improving the mechanics of the jump

I am sure everyone knows the famous Thelwell cartoon from *A Leg at Each Corner* about ponies being natural jumpers . . . Some horses are indeed natural jumpers but others do need to be taught

Ponies are natural jumpers

the art of gathering their energy and leaping into the air. The key words are balance, rhythm and impulsion. The horse finds balance by bringing his hind legs underneath him. He also needs to be able to bring his hind legs under him to take off. He must be able to bend his hocks and lower his hindquarters for this to happen. Hence, flat work will assist jumping and *vice versa*.

Jumping encourages engagement behind because unless the horse uses his hocks, he will not be able to jump. Having understood how to use himself when jumping, he can then use himself better on the flat. Provided that the rider keeps the same principles in mind, the two disciplines work hand in hand and complement each other.

To understand fully how a horse actually jumps, try jumping over something yourself. You will find that the higher the jump, the more you take shorter strides just before you launch yourself into the air as you try to gather as much energy as you can for the

but don't expect miracles too early.

leap. If you are jumping a long jump, you will run a little faster with longer strides but still take a shorter couple of steps before take-off. A horse must do exactly the same. He must arrive at the fence in balance, in rhythm (you try jumping something after changing the rhythm of your step on the run-in . . .) and with enough impulsion to jump whatever is in front of him.

One of the most important factors in any jumping is that the horse must be going forward. Free forward movement is of paramount importance at all times. It is not easy to quantify a horse 'going forward' but a variety of expressions help to describe this precious feeling: the horse should have the desire to go forward, and feels as if he wants to go half a mile an hour faster; the power (impulsion) needed to jump the fence is constrained in the rider's hand (the bigger the fence, the more power will be needed); the horse is in front of the rider's leg and up to his hand.

You can then say that if the horse is going forward, and he is balanced, you will automatically have rhythm. Rhythm is all-revealing. The moment the rhythm is lost, all is lost, for the horse will have lost impulsion and therefore balance too. Rhythm means that you have the power and balance to lengthen and shorten the stride – without rhythm, the horse is stuck in an unmanoeuvrable canter stride which, if incorrect for take-off, results in a problem.

When training your horse on the flat or over fences, one of the most important basics to establish is forward movement. If at any time this is lost, the consequences affect everything. To avoid loss of forward movement, the horse must be responsive to the rider's leg. The most common fault among riders is that they allow their horse to become 'leg dead'. You see riders' legs flapping idly against their horses' sides with the horses taking no notice. The horse must be sharp from the leg, responding to a squeeze (where the rider closes the leg using the lower half of the calf). If he does not respond, the rider must reprimand him with either a click, a flip with a whip or by the use of spurs. The horse will soon respond to the correct aid, just as he has been ignoring the leg while allowed to do so. How often does one see a rider lifting his heel for every upward transition? How often is the aid invisible, as it should be?

The most fundamental training is that legs mean 'go' and hands mean 'stop'. This is simple, but is often forgotten as the horse's training progresses. All too often problems stem from the basics – these must be established. Unless the horse responds immediately to the leg, all movements will be delayed by hesitation. There is no room for hesitation in jumping. If it takes several nudges to make the horse change from walk to trot, imagine how much leg will be necessary to jump a fence . . .

When schooling, be honest with yourself and check that when you close your leg, the horse moves willingly and fluently into the required pace. If he does not, correct him. This is obedience.

Upward and downward transitions must be without resistance and should be practised until perfect. Remember, if a horse cannot move from walk to trot, trot to canter and back again with ease, he certainly will not be able to jump from canter, increase or decrease pace in canter, let alone go faster. Smooth transitions are a sign of good balance – remember that rhythm demonstrates the power to lengthen and shorten. This is all basic schooling, sadly neglected in many instances.

The more a horse can engage his hocks and hindquarters, the more he will be able to balance himself. Exercises such as transitions, circles, changes of rein, serpentines, shoulder-in, shoulder-out, half-pass, changes of pace, rein-back and any other schooling exercise will help to improve this ability. The more supple and elastic the horse, the more athletic he will become. A stiff horse will be resistant and unable to respond to his rider's aids.

If the rider has not schooled his horse to the point where he is capable of maintaining rhythm and balance before a fence, then the horse is not ready to jump. Jumping is basic and simple. It should be a natural follow-on from flat work, where rhythm and unbalance should be established as soon as the horse commences his training as a youngster. Most riders do too much when they jump, to the detriment of the horse, and by doing too much they interfere with the basic requirements for the horse to jump his fences. So, in the same way that we take medium-length strides and then gather our energy and leap into the air, so the horse must be given the opportunity to do the same. He should jump from a rhythm and ideally take a slightly shorter stride before take-off. This final stride allows the hocks to come under him with both hind feet together for maximum spring. If the last stride is longer than the previous ones, the horse will be unable to gather his energy and the jump will be flat and unbalanced. The higher and more difficult the jump, the more crucial is the need for the approach to be correct and the take-off precise. A young horse should not be expected to jump big fences until his training allows him to approach his fences correctly. If he should arrive at a big fence unbalanced and not in a position to jump it, he will be forced into making a serious mistake. This can easily upset his confidence so that instead of enjoying his jumping, he starts to worry and become nervous.

Balance is crucial on the approach and take-off. The horse must arrive at the fence with a light forehand. He has to lift this up – first by pushing off with his front legs and then by powering from behind. If the horse is heavy on his forehand (i.e. unbalanced) he will not be able to lift himself (and his rider) over the fence. A knock-down, refusal or fall will be the result. The less perfect the horse's technique, the more important it is that the balance is established, otherwise the horse will have no chance of clearing any fence.

In the same way that we use our arms to help our balance, a horse uses his head and neck. If, on the approach to a fence, the horse's head and neck are restricted, it is extremely difficult for him to jump the fence. Imagine, yourself, running towards a jump with your arms tied to your sides, only released at the very last moment. This is the sensation a horse suffers from when his rider insists that he approaches the fences in what is commonly thought of as a 'dressage shape'. If you watch a horse jumping loose, you will notice how he lowers and lengthens his neck slightly on the last couple of strides of the approach. He does this without losing balance and is then free to use his head and neck to the maximum over the fence. The suppleness of the horse's back is dependent upon the looseness of the neck, and should the neck be tight, so the back will be the same.

If the horse is allowed to approach his fences in a natural outline, he will find jumping so much easier than if he is forced into a tight shape with his nose vertical to the ground (see Figure 11). Just because the horse is not in the conventional 'dressage' shape, it does not mean that he is not on his hocks or balanced. (Dressage is balance within a frame; jumping is just balance.) It is a pity that so many event riders have a misconceived idea of how to ride a horse to a fence. They fail to understand the easiest way for their horse to jump and assume that because they gain good dressage marks they should ride their horses exactly the same when jumping. The Americans have perfected the 'natural outline' and work their horses much more towards that end. The British seem to be far more intent upon aiming for their horses to be 'on the bit' – a generally misunderstood term, interpreted by the horse's head being held in an unnatural position, with the nose vertical. This points to the fact that many riders ride back to front in that they do not ride the horse from behind into the hand, so never obtain true connection of energy generated from behind into the hand.

As is always the case when trying to grasp an idea, try watching the *top* riders (not the second division) in both show-jumping and eventing and study how they present their horses to a fence. If you question whether a Grade A show-jumper is comparable to a

11. This horse is on the last couple of strides before a fence. The rider is in forward position with her seat in the saddle, although she is not sitting heavily. She is using her seat to keep the horse coming forward to the fence and is staying in balance to take off. She has allowed the horse to stretch his head and neck to allow maximum freedom for take-off. You can see that the horse is bringing his hocks well under him and the impression is of the weight being on the hindquarters and not on the forehand.

Note the general outline prior to take-off. Imagine how much change in outline would be required if the horse were in a dressage shape on the approach. Imagine also how much change of balance there would be if the horse had to make such an alteration. Given the restriction a horse would feel when he knows that this is the natural shape he has to be in to jump a fence, it is little surprise that he sometimes tries to take matters into his own hands to relieve himself of this restriction by shoving his head in the air and rushing to the fence . . . Is it not an all too common mistake?

Note here the straight lines from the rider's toe, knee, elbow and shoulder – a perpendicular line dropped would pass through all those points – and a similarly straight line from the horse's mouth through the hand and elbow. An unusual shot, and an interesting one from which to learn.

novice event horse, watch Mark Todd when he rides both types of horse and see in what sort of outline he rides them when jumping. When eventing, it is necessary to be adaptable and teach your horse how to carry himself *correctly* in both 'dressage' and jumping outlines. For this reason I prefer to think of flat work and jumping, rather than dressage and jumping, going hand in hand.

All too often one sees a rider shortening the horse's stride on the approach and then sending the horse to the fence on a one, two, three basis. The poor horse, restricted on the approach, is then flung onto his forehand and expected to jump the fence. Some horses learn to cope with this way of being ridden and eventually learn self-preservation. Others cannot cope and end up refusing, hitting fences or even falling. Unfortunately some riders have not progressed from their Pony Club days when their ponies tolerated being ridden like this, basically ignoring their riders and jumping in spite of them. Horses need more assistance from us as riders, but this must be assistance in the form of correct riding, not interfering riding. Correct riding is allowing the horse to approach his fences in a balanced, rhythmical pace where the horse is carrying himself on his hocks and not on his rider's hand. The rider must remain in balance himself and sit still. All the aids should be soft and light and the horse should appear to spring effortlessly over his fences with invisible aids from the rider. The rider must stay in perfect balance, not moving his body until the horse takes off. He must be light with his hands and allow the horse total freedom with his head and neck over the fence. If the horse has impulsion stored in his hocks, the rider will contain this in his hand. In some cases the horse may be quite strong in the hand, but this is stored energy and not a case of the horse finding balance in the rider's hand. The rider should be able to soften the contact slightly on the last couple of strides to allow the horse to lengthen and lower his head and neck before take-off. This does not mean dropping the horse and losing contact completely. You do see some top show-jumpers losing contact before take-off, but they are riding schooled horses. They have very accurate eyes for strides and can place their horses precisely for take-off. The horses are given total freedom of their heads and necks just prior to take-off when jumping big fences, so there is no restriction at all on how much they can use themselves (which must be to the maximum over a very big fence). The riders hold their horses with their legs and, being totally obedient, the horses understand and obey their riders' wishes. A young horse can take advantage of no contact by running out. The uneven terrain of cross-country means that the horse must be between the rider's hand and leg at all times to stay in balance. The terrain on a show-jumping arena is normally flat and easier for the horse to keep his balance on.

If he is in balance, the horse will not alter his rhythm or fall onto his forehand. He will merely follow through with an elastic, supple jump, using himself to the maximum. Any restriction or tightness from the rider will prevent this. The horse must also be allowed to follow his jump through and the rider must allow freedom with the rein until the horse has landed and found his own balance. If the rider takes up the contact too soon, the horse will hollow on landing in anticipation and this stiffness will affect the approach to the next fence. It may also cause the horse to hit fences behind.

As much premium is placed on the rider's balance as the horse's. A rider finds his balance by the security of his seat and by the true weight sitting firmly on the stirrup at all times. The rider's position is the way of communicating the aids to the horse. A secure seat is an independent seat with the rider at no time, especially in emergencies, relying on the reins for balance. The moment the weight is no longer on the stirrup, the rider loses his security and balance. He is then relying on the horse to keep himself in position. This is disconcerting for the horse and increases the difficulty for him in keeping his own balance. A rider's loss of balance really upsets a nervy young horse. A difficult horse to break is super-sensitive to rider movement and change of balance, and should the rider be out of balance for a moment, the horse's immediate reaction is to gallop off or to try to remove his rider. The very good rider is the one who can keep an independent balance even in critical moments, but of course this is the moment when most riders do lose it and rely totally on the horse. If the crisis is due to the horse making a mistake himself, he will not be there to help the rider, so disaster follows. If the horse makes a mistake and the rider is still in balance, the horse can often recover his own balance and a problem is averted. An unbalanced rider can actually make a horse fall should the horse lose balance himself, for example pecking on landing.

Standing up in the stirrups makes the rider aware of his balance – or lack of it! Riding without stirrups and reins helps to improve balance, and being lunged over a fence without reins is good practice, provided you have someone experienced doing the lungeing. The greatest art when riding to a fence is being able to *keep still* – not only by not interfering with the reins but by keeping still with the body so that the horse is left alone and

uninhibited. Try giving someone a piggy back who is wriggling around – you will soon tell them to keep still. Horses cannot speak . . .

Every sport requires balance and skill. Riding is even more difficult because there is an animate object to cope with as well. Horses jumping loose rarely make mistakes – we as riders must give our horses a chance to perform as if they were loose. We have to teach them how to cope with the change in their balance caused by our weight being on their backs and to give them the confidence that they will encounter no restriction even when they make a mistake.

Unless we train our horses and ourselves too, we cannot expect good results. This training must be thoroughly established with the basics correct. The horse must go freely forwards in a calm manner. He must be able to maintain a good rhythm throughout and be straight. (This means that the hind feet follow the track made by the front feet and that the horse bends around his corners and is straight on the straight.) As his training progresses, so his hocks should come further under him so that his balance improves accordingly. He should be capable of extending and collecting, and, during all transitions as well as in each pace, he should accept the bit without resistance.

Jumping should be introduced to the young horse in the form of poles on the ground, trotting poles and little fences to be jumped from trot. All this may be done at an early stage, executed in conjunction with the same level of flat work at the time. Trotting poles will help to improve the balance and rhythm by forcing the hocks and joints to bend and so increasing the suppleness.*

The most important thing to teach any horse is to pick up the rhythm as soon as he has landed over a fence. He will then learn automatically to canter in rhythm and balance, so making the approach to the next fence easier. If a horse is allowed to land and 'die' when working at home, he will be difficult to ride at a show when jumping a course. In the early stages, the horse must be allowed just to jump fences out of the rhythm. It is only when the horse is capable of lengthening and shortening his stride without losing rhythm that the rider can, if necessary, alter the canter on the approach. Initially the horse will jump off a rather long stride because this is the only canter he can manage. The moment the rider tries to force a shorter canter, he will be restricting the horse and stopping the forward movement. This then encourages the

12. The horse has arrived too close to the fence for a comfortable take-off and has dropped a leg. Horse and rider quickly restored balance to continue unhindered. Note the 'defensive' lower leg position in the second photo and how the horse has been allowed total freedom of his head and neck.

*This is all discussed in detail in *The Less-Than-Perfect Horse.*

horse to rush and increase the pace to avoid the restriction. Only as the flat work progresses can the jumping progress and improve.

It is important that practice fences both at home and in the collecting ring at a competition are well built. A horse will not be encouraged to jump well over a flimsy, poorly presented obstacle, which will invite careless, inattentive jumping. In the ring, a well-built course is one which uses plenty of fillers with big, solid-looking poles in bold colours. Although horses are colour blind, they do seem to be able to differentiate between bright colours and pale ones. Something imposing gives the horse more to look at and sets him up. As he takes note of the fence, it has the effect of putting more weight on his hindquarters and lightening his forehand. He is then in the correct carriage to jump the fence well, whereas if he spooks and backs off so much that he stops going forward, he may well refuse or knock down the fence.

The skill in building fences from only poles is to provide an inviting fence which helps the horse to throw a good jump. A good jump is dependent upon the point of take-off. It is difficult for a horse to judge his take-off at a vertical fence, but a pole placed approximately 1–2 feet in front of the fence prevents him from getting too close. This pole helps the horse to back off – i.e. shorten his last stride – to ensure a springy jump. The fence can be filled in with a diagonal drop pole and made more imposing by having two poles very close together to give a more solid appearance as a top line.

Another method of encouraging a horse to back off is to use Vs. These are not permitted in the collecting ring at the practice fence but do play a useful role at home. The closer together the points on the pole, the more effect the Vs will have. (It is worth bearing in mind the effect of poles placed in this way when it comes to assessing cross-country fences.) Vs are most usefully employed on a vertical fence, although if a horse consistently runs too deep to a parallel (although normally the parallel, being a spread fence, is enough to make a horse look and set himself up) a V can be used.

If a horse jumps crooked, a high cross-pole as the front of a spread will help to keep him straight on his approach and prevent him from twisting in the air.

Due to their more imposing nature, spread fences are easier to jump than uprights. A parallel with a diagonal drop pole offers a solid, well-built obstacle. An ascending spread is a more inviting and easier obstacle, especially for a young horse, but for the older horse it is almost too easy and invites a flat jump because the horse does not have to use himself to the full.

The types of fences to avoid building are flimsy, gappy ones where the horse has nothing to respect or judge. You do not want your horse to be frightened of poles or a fence, but he should respect anything at which he is presented. A good person on the ground is one who can decide what type of fence a horse requires to improve his jump at any given moment. This person has to be experienced and have a deep-rooted knowledge of jumping to be astute enough to help. When putting up the practice fence for a horse, it is necessary to be observant so that you do not present a horse with a false ground-line or an uninviting fence which may cause a bad jump. Someone on the ground who can help at a practice fence can make all the difference between a clear round and faults in the ring.

If at home your horse is being sloppy and careless, it often helps to introduce a filler or different type of fence to make the horse look at what he is doing. If his attention is drawn to the fence, the horse should make more effort. Jumping fences on the angle can also make the horse sharpen up, take more notice and make more effort. But you might just need to give the horse a break from jumping for a while so that he comes back fresh to his task.

Some horses are naturally more careful than others. It is rare to find a horse who is bold enough to jump the most imposing looking cross-country fences yet careful enough never to touch a coloured pole. However, the truly clumsy horse is unusual and on the whole horses do not like to hit fences. I discuss in detail the reasons for horses hitting fences in *The Less-Than-Perfect Horse*, but lack of training and poor presentation at a fence are normally the basic reasons. If the horse arrives at a fence with neither rhythm, balance nor impulsion, he will have little option but to make a poor jump which will probably be rewarded with penalties. The less perfect the horse's natural balance and also technique over a fence, the more vital this correct presentation must be. This is the reason why a good horse is easier to ride than a moderate one. A good horse will have naturally good balance and therefore be able to adjust his stride with ease. The moderate horse will lack natural balance and therefore be unable to organise himself for take-off. Claims on the rider's ability and effectiveness will be far greater from the moderate horse. The good horse could jump with the proverbial monkey perched on his back! Motto – try to choose a well-balanced horse rather than one who, even with schooling, will be unable to carry himself.

When schooling at home over fences, the rider should alternate between using grids and exercises, and jumping fences from canter. All too often, riders use only grids, lulling themselves into a false sense of security, hiding in the safety of a grid. A grid is useful as a schooling aid and will help to supple a horse and correct his jump, but the ultimate aim is to be able to canter around a course of fences and a grid will not help directly either you or the horse in that respect, so make sure that you do jump a variety of fences from canter.

When schooling at home you should jump single fences, related-distance fences with three, four or even five strides between, fences on the angle and a number of related fences all on the angle, turning in short and turning short afterwards. In other words, train and discipline your horse to answer your aids. Do not wait until you go to a show to practise turning short to a fence or jumping angled fences. This technique should be perfected at home. The fences you practise over need not be big, but merely obstacles to ensure that you ride and present the horse correctly. Tiny fences can invite sloppy riding and even if the horse is badly presented will cause no problems. Invariably it is the rider who needs 'sharpening up' and it is important that the horse is not the victim of poor riding. So, if you yourself are riding or you are helping someone, prevent problems by making sure that you or your pupil are riding correctly even over a one-foot fence.

Jumping requires practice. Obviously you do not want to jump your horse every day, but popping over a fence several times a week is good for a young horse who is learning how to jump. I would alternate what he jumps, i.e. an exercise, single fences, ditches and water (in the case of an event horse) so that he is kept sharp and alert. If you jump the same things every day, the horse soon becomes bored and complacent and you will encourage him to be idle and careless.

A young horse should never learn the word 'refusal', for once he has discovered that the easy way out is to stop, this will become a bad habit which is also demoralising for the rider and will cause him to ride badly. Similarly, you should also avoid knock-downs. A young horse will often jump extravagantly over new fences, but quickly becomes tired and loses his spring. If you persist in jumping the same thing over and over again, the horse will become bored, will learn that tapping poles does not hurt and will cease to have respect for his fences.

Throughout the training of a horse, it is up to the rider not only to present his horse correctly at each and every fence but also never to ask his horse to jump a fence which is too big or difficult for his stage of training. There is a real skill in producing a confident horse who never doubts his own ability or that of his rider. If a horse is given a fright, particularly at the start of his jumping career, he may quickly lose heart in something which hitherto he has found fun. Horses should enjoy jumping. Few horses will jump on their own for fun – fortunately, otherwise we would have problems keeping them in fields – but once they have learnt how to jump, they seem to like it. It is important that this attitude is nurtured and if the horse shows any signs of doubt, the rider must ask himself where the problem lies. It could be fright, boredom or a reluctance to jump which stems from physical discomfort or illness. It is important to establish the cause of any loss of performance before continuing jumping, for jumping may aggravate it.

It is never easy to know how quickly to progress with a horse in his jumping. As a general rule, the horse will indicate when he is ready to jump bigger and more demanding fences. It can be a mistake to spend too long jumping tiny fences. Once a horse has his confidence, he must learn 'how' to jump. Very small fences do not encourage a horse to 'jump'. They do not require him to jump from his hocks and be neat with his forelegs, for he can scramble over a tiny fence. He may then become idle and complacent about jumping, and, if this happens, it often comes as a rude awakening when he has to jump higher. It may then take several knock-downs before the horse realises that he must make more effort.

Grids and exercises

A very green horse is difficult to ride over a fence, particularly if he has never jumped anything before. This is where loose jumping can be of enormous benefit. Although not essential, it helps the horse to learn how to look after himself and to alter his stride for take-off, and most horses enjoy it.

A loose jumping area is invaluable when training horses. This may be a fenced-off area specifically for loose jumping or a small indoor school. If the area is too big, it is too difficult to control the horse, but a larger indoor school can be cordoned off with jump wings and poles. To loose jump a horse well is an art. It requires experience and knowledge because it is not merely a case of shooing a horse round a school over a fence. The 'groundman' must be able to anticipate the horse's every move and be ready with his voice or the whip to maintain rhythm and forward movement, at the same time ensuring that the whole procedure is done with the horse happy and relaxed. It is of no benefit to the horse's schooling programme if he is nervous, galloping flat out round the school and jumping haphazardly over fences.

Watching a horse loose jumped well is a pleasure. Without the rider's weight (and, sadly, in many cases the interference and hindrance of a rider), the horse finds jumping much easier. He learns how to control himself on take-off and discovers the mechanics required to jump. When the rider is back on board, the horse will not necessarily jump as well as when he is loose, but at least he has learnt the technique of jumping and then only has to master how to re-balance himself with the added weight of the rider.

Jumping on the lunge without a rider is not as beneficial for the horse as jumping completely loose. The horse is perpetually on the turn and invariably hangs on the lunge-line, which affects his self-carriage. The proximity of the person on the ground does unsettle some horses and they cannot concentrate so well on their jumping. It is difficult to lunge well over a fence and sometimes more damage than good is done. As a result, it is preferable to teach a horse how to jump by using grids rather than lungeing.

Grids and exercises are essential to improve the horse's jump. There are a myriad different combinations of poles and fences, but it is always useful to start with some basic ones.

The basic grid of trotting from a trot pole to a parallel (see Diagram 1) – 8 feet from trot pole to cross-pole followed by a pole 9 feet away, then a further 9 feet to a parallel – is one of the most useful when teaching a young horse to jump. The horse is guided to the correct points for take-off by the various poles, which not only gives him confidence but also puts him in a perfect take-off position, giving him the best opportunity to jump well. The cross-pole guides the horse to the centre of the grid and makes him jump straight. Similarly, crossed poles as the first rail of the parallel have the same function. The front rail of the parallel should eventually be put straight, so forming a true parallel. The horse is then put in a situation where he must be quick to fold his forelegs and jump off his hocks, then use himself behind to clear the back rail. This exercise is useful for young as well as experienced horses because the difficulty can vary quite considerably.

Extra fences can be added onto this basic grid. Uprights or oxers can be placed at different distances beyond the grid to add to the complexity of the exercise. The distances should remain short to ensure that the horse uses himself to the maximum, but should not be so short that the horse is tempted to miss out strides, so it may have to vary for each individual horse and its stage of training. An experienced horse is better able to alter and shorten than a green horse. It is important to avoid the sort of mishap which can occur when an oxer is three or four strides away from the grid on a shortish distance and a young, inexperienced horse tries to miss out a stride. The likelihood is that he will land in the middle of the fence, giving himself an enormous fright or even injuring himself. It is important to have someone experienced to help when working a horse through shortened distances. That person will recognise early signs of a horse's reaction to various distances and will have the foresight to avoid a possible problem.

An exercise which I have found useful for both horse and rider is a line of, say, four trotting poles at 4.5 feet apart, then 9 feet to a small cross-pole. This teaches a rider how to sit still on the approach and how, by doing so, he preserves the balance. If the rider moves too much with his body, or interferes with the horse by driving him forward out of rhythm, the horse will not be able to trot over the poles without tapping them and will be unable to meet the cross-pole correctly.

It is a good exercise to use to teach a rider to maintain the impulsion without losing rhythm or balance and also how to wait for the fence. The horse remains in balance then and is able to meet the fence correctly. He must be quick on his feet and, should he try to rush to the fence, he will have an uncomfortable jump. Having felt how easily the horse copes with this exercise when done correctly, the rider should try to apply the same principles when jumping a fence from canter. The line of trotting poles increases activity in the hocks without any action on the part of the rider – so in canter the rider must use his legs to maintain that same impulsion. The trotting poles keep the horse in balance, so in canter the rider must ensure that he does not allow the horse's stride to get longer as he uses his legs. The trotting poles set the horse up for the fence and encourage the balance to stay the same until take-off – in canter the rider must keep his own body still to help the horse keep his balance all the way to the fence. This is a particularly useful exercise for any rider who finds it difficult not to 'throw' his horse at the fence at the last minute.

Throughout all exercises, the rider must allow the horse full freedom of his head and neck. Any restriction or tightness in the neck on the approach or over the fence will adversely affect the jump by causing stiffness throughout. If you watch how a horse jumps, it will then make sense to you to allow the horse to approach his fences in a natural outline. If the rider tries to approach a fence with his horse's nose vertical (i.e. in a dressage outline), the horse has to make a dramatic change of outline as he takes off. Most horses fight this restriction from their riders and start rushing in the last few strides. If the horse is allowed to arrive in a free, unconstrained outline, he is already in a shape for jumping and can bascule over his fences without any undue change of shape.

A useful exercise to encourage a horse to jump off his hocks is a vertical with a trot pole in front at 8 feet. The horse should be trotted slowly to this fence on a very light contact so that he cannot jump out of his rider's hand. He has to jump off his hocks. A pole on landing side at 9 feet further encourages the horse to bascule as he looks down at the pole. This also helps a horse who jumps out too far, so unbalancing himself for the next fence. Generally a horse who jumps out too far is not jumping off his hocks, but is lurching himself over a fence, so this exercise helps twofold.

Exercises are beneficial and, used in moderation, help both horse and rider. It is equally beneficial to jump fences from trot and canter without the assistance of placing poles. There are no placing poles to be found in a competition! Furthermore, it is against BSJA rules to use placing poles in the collecting ring at a show or event, so it is important to be able to work a horse without needing any.

Jumping should always be a spectacle of lightness and ease stemming from balance, rhythm and impulsion. The rider's hand should be soft, allowing the horse to use himself athletically without restriction and interference. When loose, a horse jumps with consummate ease. He can alter his stride and jump out of a rhythm with little problem. It is vital that we do not create problems for the horse by interfering to the detriment of his performance. We are there to help the horse, not to dominate him. Alas, it is a rare sight to see a harmonious picture of horse and rider jumping a course of fences. The horse must be well-trained and disciplined (there is a difference between discipline and domination) for this to be possible. So many riders spend hours working on their dressage. What they fail to do in so many cases is put that dressage into practice when jumping. If the dressage falls apart as soon as the horse jumps a fence, then I'm afraid the dressage is not correct. The ultimate aim of all dressage or flat work (as I prefer to think of it) is for the horse to carry himself in balance. If at any time the horse is relying on your hand, or you are relying on your hand to hold the horse in position, then you know that you are cheating. The horse must stay in position or shape by carrying himself on his hocks and hindquarters. Unless he does this correctly, he will not be able to balance himself or find impulsion when necessary.

To produce a horse who is going correctly, it is necessary for the rider to ride correctly. To summarise what makes a good rider, one could say that it is balance, feel and rhythm. From this, the rider is most effective; he has 'good hands' and can use his legs to good effect. 'Feel' comes from experience and an understanding of what one should expect from a horse. Balance – which comes from a secure lower leg with the weight firmly in the heel at all times – is paramount, and the higher the standard attained, the more delicate the balance becomes.

Exercises

For all grid exercises, the rider must stay in balance, keep an even rhythm and not get in front of his horse. Check your position – hollow loin, heels down, head up, hip angle closed. The grid can be raised to a suitable height for the standard of horse/pupil.

● 1. *Introducing the young horse to a grid*
Trotting poles teach balance and rhythm and aid suppleness.

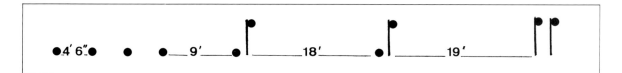

Introduce a low cross-pole 9 feet away. Concentrate on keeping in balance with the horse, maintaining rhythm and ensuring that the horse does not miss out a trot step. Change the cross-pole to a small vertical. Introduce a second jump of cross-pole, changing the first element back to a cross-pole for the first attempt. Then change both elements to verticals. Introduce a third element of crossed poles for a spread, cross first and second elements. Gradually raise to verticals and a true parallel.

● 2. *Bounces*
Bounces are useful suppling exercises and can easily be incorporated into grids. This one is a simple introduction demanding

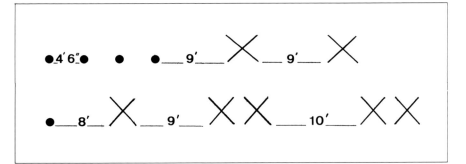

control, rhythm and balance. The rider should follow the light contact on the horse's mouth and make minimum body movement – the more upper body movement, the more unbalancing it is for the horse and the more likely the rider is to get in front of the movement.

● 3. *Improving the turn*

This exercise was shown to me by Jimmy Wofford, a four-times Olympic rider and now a leading American coach. Starting on the horse's better rein, the rider should canter a circle and jump one of the elements on the circle. He should then miss out the next one and jump alternate elements. When he is ready, he should jump

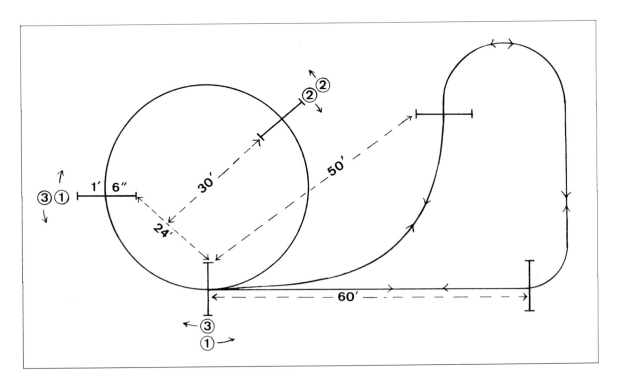

all three elements. Start the full circle with a jump that has the greater distance to the next element. He must concentrate on keeping the rhythm and staying in balance. If there is an option of strides, he should opt for the shorter one. If the horse lands on the wrong leg or breaks into trot, jump the next element from trot and pick up the canter again from the jump. If the horse knocks down a fence, carry on and jump the poles on the ground (unless scattered) until it is put up again. Maintain rhythm and balance and keep looking ahead all the time. Just allow the horse to jump and remain as passive and still as possible with the upper body.

● 4. *Increasing athleticism*
This is a variation on the theme of no. 1, but gives a longer distance between trotting poles and cross-pole, followed by a shorter distance to a parallel, then a short two strides and a short three strides. The higher the fences, the tighter the distance becomes. For the rider, it is a test of balance and position, allowing the horse to jump up underneath you, with minimum movement from yourself.

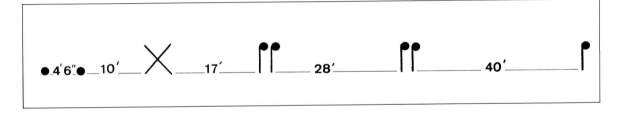

● 5. *Related distances*
The horse should be able to jump the two fences on an even five strides. In between elements you must go with your horse – if you get behind him, it will have the effect of sending him on (which is the principle in getting 'behind your horse' when approaching difficult cross-country fences like water, coffins or drops). By being behind the movement, you send the horse in front of you. In a short distance, this is counter-productive. You must stay with

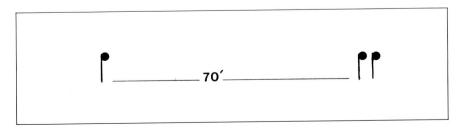

39

the horse and shorten him by holding and closing the hand rather than by using body weight.

Only if the horse tries to rush should you then stop him with a closed hand. If he lands over one element and 'waits for the grab', it will have the effect of making him try to make a dash for it. If the rider is passive and non-interfering, the horse will be able to jump as if loose.

The same line should be jumped in six strides, again keeping the rhythm but holding to shorten the stride to get in an extra one.

These sorts of exercises are important and horses must be obedient to the rider's wishes. Make sure you keep your eyes up and practise continuing the canter afterwards by, for example, riding a circle.

● 6. *Changing direction and turning*
The more experienced horse should be able to make a flying change. The event horse should be able to stay in balance in counter-canter if he cannot change. The circle afterwards is practice for picking up a good canter before making another turn to a combination. It should be repeated on both reins.

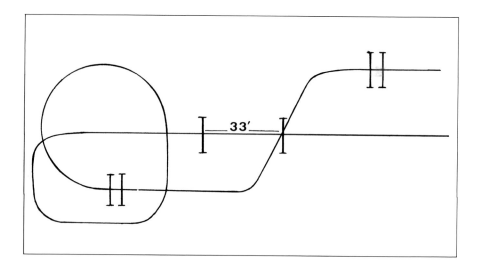

● 7. *Turning short to a fence off either rein*
The rider must keep his eyes ahead and look round each turn. The horse must stay in rhythm and balance. It is good practice for a rider to change from two-point position to three-point on the corners when he must sit up (see below, page 46). The jumping seat should alternate in this way and here is a good exercise to

experiment with this. The
change of seat should not
affect the horse's rhythm.

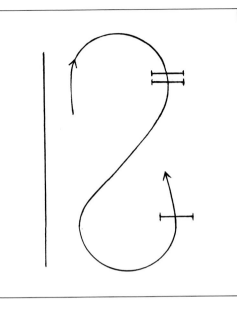

● 8. *Improving the turn
and balance*
This serpentine with fences
on the centre line is an
advanced exercise which
improves turning, balance,
speed of reaction and the
ability to change legs.

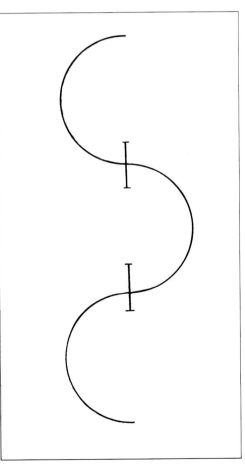

● *9.   Changing legs*
An exercise to improve the turn and to teach the horse how to change legs by cantering a figure of eight over a pole on the ground. The rider should use an open rein to the inside to guide the horse and neck rein with the outside hand. The rider can also set his outside hand and turn with his inside. Either way is correct and the horse should learn to respond to both.

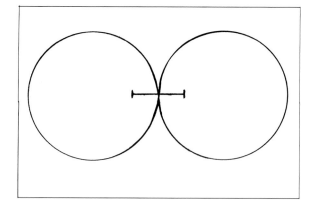

● *10.   Jumping one fence after another*

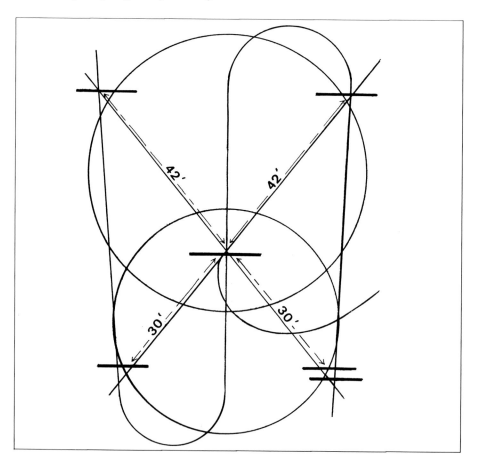

This construction of fences has a variety of options. You can jump two or three related distances on the angle. You can jump fences straight on with a tight turn up the centre. You can jump two fences on a circle. The permutations are endless and give ample opportunity to keep jumping, practising picking up rhythm and balance immediately. Provided the fences are small, a young horse can work through this exercise in readiness for jumping a course of fences. The distances can be altered as necessary to suit the height of fences.

Grids are a means to an end and are invaluable in producing a well-schooled horse, but all these grids should be kept small and not used either for too long or too often. Jumping is tiring for a young horse and he can soon lose the benefit of the exercises by being tired and starting to flop over his fences.

It is useful to jump in a group of people because changing a grid for one horse is tiresome. It also gives the horses a chance to have a breather while the others have their turn. Watching other horses and riders can only be beneficial, if only to avoid the traps they fall into!

At all times, you are trying to improve your horse's balance and rhythm and to make him more obedient – this is the object of all schooling. Work hard to perfect your own position, and therefore balance, too. Grids give ample opportunity for this – once you are in the security of a grid, there is nothing else to worry about. Grids and lines of fences in related distances also help to teach the rider to feel rhythm and to improve his eye for a stride.

The rider's position and technique

The jumping position involves the forward seat. The weight, as always, should be firmly in the heels, with the upper body inclined forward and little weight on the seat bones. The aids are hands, legs and weight, rather than seat – after all, a jockey never uses his seat but utilises weight displacement, i.e. balance. If the rider sits heavily in the saddle, he is not encouraging the horse to be loose in his back and indeed may cause the horse to hollow. If the body is 100 per cent upright, the rider is likely to be behind the movement, and in order to catch up with it he has to make a dramatic lunge with the forward swing to keep in balance. As with any throwing of weight, this is unbalancing for the horse and may affect the jump by putting extra weight onto the horse's shoulders.

13. A loose seat can result in a problem. Although in the first two pictures the horses are jumping the fence well, neither rider has weight in the heel and both are looking down, which suggests that neither would survive a serious mistake from the horse.

The result is shown in this sequence through a combination. From the first shot, all looks well. The rider is in a good position, head up, body upright, although the reins could be rather long. The horse has half his attention on the fence ahead (note one ear back). The following photos show the horse having hit the final element and causing a true case of UR (unseated rider). In the first 'emergency' picture, the rider is relying on the horse's neck for his balance and the lower leg is not braced against the stirrup. The horse has hit the fence hard and has twisted, making the moment very unseating. However, the subsequent UR might have been averted had the rider had his heel down, the lower leg totally secure and his body and head up. When the horse twists like this, it is vital that the rider counterbalances by using the diagonal stirrup. This rider, having failed to do so, paid the penalty.

14. Two riders behind the movement. The first one is 'hailing a cab'. The horse has obviously required a smack on the approach. The rider is in a good defensive position and is in behind her horse, with a secure lower leg, head up and shoulders back. It is important to try to get the hand back on the rein as quickly as possible and certainly before the horse lands. With the reins in one hand, the horse can easily be unbalanced or pulled to one side, which may cause a run-out. If you hit the horse, try to replace your hand on the rein immediately. Make it second nature to do this when at home so that you will automatically do it in a competition.

The second rider is behind the horse to the extent that she is too far behind the movement. In order to catch up, she will have to throw her body weight forward over any subsequent element, which is unbalancing for the horse. This horse has his ears pricked even though he seems restricted in his neck.

The event rider must be able to adopt the 'safety seat' – in which the lower leg moves forward as the foot is braced against the stirrup – should the horse make a mistake or peck on landing.

There are times in both cross-country and show-jumping when it is necessary for the rider to be behind his horse if he feels that the horse might stop. This is less likely to happen in a show-jumping arena once a horse has become accustomed to the various types of fence and filler. Cross-country fences, however, conceal various hazards and surprises for the horse, such as ditches, changes of terrain or water, so the rider has to ensure that he stays *behind* the horse until he has actually taken off. In normal circumstances in show-jumping, the rider should stay *with* his horse and be neither in front nor behind. The good event rider is the one who can adapt from one occasion to another and is not stereotyped as always being behind his horse or not being able to adapt to that position when necessary.

Whether the rider has some weight or no weight on the seat depends on the horse, the occasion or the preference of the rider. The Americans call it two-point position when there is no weight on the seat and three-point when the rider engages the seat (though not sitting heavily in the saddle). The three-point position is normally adopted on a turn or on any occasion when the horse needs to be re-balanced and set onto his hocks or driven forward – i.e. before any cross-country fence. A change of balance is necessary here, and if it is a difficult fence, the rider must stay in behind the horse. An experienced rider can switch from one position to another without being conscious of doing so. It is an automatic reaction to a moment.

The most important aspect of position is that the rider should *never* get *in front* of his horse. There should be no reason why a rider should get in front of his horse more from a forward position than from an upright one. The crucial factor is any *change* of position – and therefore balance – before a fence. Upper body movement invites the rider to get in front of the balance. The rider must retain whatever position he has until the horse takes off. This is why it is so difficult for the rider to stay with the horse if he is in a totally upright position on take-off, as he needs to be very quick to catch up with the movement.

We are all taught forward swing from an early age and sometimes we overdo the swing. We should allow the horse's jump to close the angle of the hip and not fling our weight onto the horse's withers and neck. Apart from the unbalancing factor, we are also relying on the horse's neck for security, rather than the

15. Compare two riders in similar take-off positions. The first rider is in front of her horse and therefore in front of the movement. This is a dangerous position in which to be and should be avoided at all costs. Always stay behind your horse at a difficult fence. Although you can stay with him at an easy one, be in a position to get behind if necessary. The second rider has total security in the lower leg and heel and is with her horse in balance over a simple fence. Neither horse is tidy with its front legs — they have been slow to fold. Note the bend and strain on the hocks of the first horse and the push coming from behind from both horses.

16. This is an uncomfortable looking moment. The rider is too far behind the movement and is relying on the reins for her balance. The horse is not being given the opportunity to use his head and neck for his balance. It may be that the balance was not good before take-off and this is the result. One can see that if there were subsequent elements to jump, a problem could well result.

weight being in the heel. If the horse should make a mistake, or peck, we have no security left and may either cause the horse to fall by unbalancing him, or will probably fall off. Mark Phillips gives a good explanation of this 'collapsing' by demonstrating with his hand on a whip (see Diagram 11). If the rider swings too far forward as the horse takes off, he is in effect pushing the horse's shoulder down. As the horse takes off, he automatically causes a forward swing so the rider only needs to keep the hip angle closed and the correct jumping position is automatically created. Many riders, including successful ones, do not have a good jumping seat. They may bring the heel up continually or swing to one side or the other. The best riders have a good security of the lower leg and are always in perfect balance. A well-balanced rider is a light rider who will never resort to the horse's back or the reins to preserve his balance.

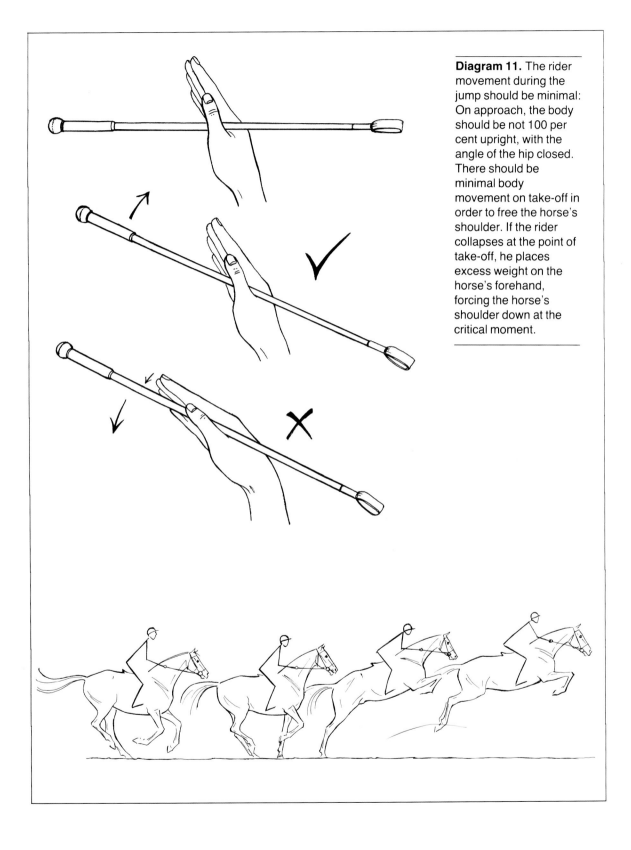

Diagram 11. The rider movement during the jump should be minimal: On approach, the body should be not 100 per cent upright, with the angle of the hip closed. There should be minimal body movement on take-off in order to free the horse's shoulder. If the rider collapses at the point of take-off, he places excess weight on the horse's forehand, forcing the horse's shoulder down at the critical moment.

Good hands come from good balance. Sympathetic hands and feel come from experience, although a natural talent does affect this sensitivity. The rider should carry his hands above and in front of the horse's withers. If the hands are held too low, the arm will be straight and therefore stiff. The horse will resist this stiffness and he will react adversely because the bit will be acting on the bars of the mouth as opposed to the corners. A soft, relaxed elbow is crucial to the whole action of the hand and arm. Similarly, the wrist should not be turned flat – it should be thought of as a continuation of the arm. In this way it will stay soft and supple, whereas if it bends in, out or down, it will immediately stiffen.

17. This is an impressive series of pictures showing Mark Todd not surviving a mistake at Belton despite his excellent position throughout. Note how in the second frame the horse is being given full use of his neck in order to give him every chance of recovering from his mistake. At the same time, the rider's shoulders are starting to come back in a defensive attitude. Once the point of no return is reached, the rider tries to keep his balance by letting go of the reins to allow his shoulders to come further back. From his position in the final frame, the rider will be thrown clear and the horse will not roll on him. If the rider's weight had been too far forward, he would have stayed with the horse too long and fallen under him.

18. It is important for the correct position to be second nature. If you get into the bad habits seen in some of these photos, when the time comes for the 'safety seat' it will not be there, as is shown here. The horse has hit the fence, but not so badly that a fall is obvious from the first photo. The rider's weight, being too far forward, is influencing the balance and the partnership looks as if it is coming to grief. Had the rider been sitting further back, he might have been able to influence the balance more.

19. From the position of the horse's front legs, it is clear that he is struggling to clear the spread. The rider is giving the horse complete freedom of his head and neck to give him every opportunity to stretch and reach forward. If the rider were out of balance, he would be unable to do this and would have to find his balance on the horse's mouth. This in turn would cause a restriction which would prevent the horse from clearing the fence.

All too often we tell riders to relax. Of course, if we relaxed completely we would fall off. A better expression would be to try to lengthen your back or imagine someone has hold of the top of your hat and is trying to lift you higher. That idea for posture, coupled with imagining that your arms are very light and full of air, should create the necessary feeling of good posture without tension. The rider who naturally carries her or himself in an elegant way when walking around will have an advantage over the naturally sloppy person.

The lower back should be slightly hollow to enable the rider to lighten his seat. The main weight of the rider should be in the front half of the saddle and the actual bearing points should be the thighs and through the lower leg to the heel. It should not be the horse's back which takes the weight. This is, of course, much harder work than sitting in a saddle as if it were a chair. The best demonstration of the correct, balanced position would be if you could pull the horse out from underneath the rider and he landed on his feet and did not drop back onto his bottom (see Diagram 12). The more perfect the position, the better the balance and the more effective the rider will be. As in any sport, the better the technique, the better the player.

Under the same category as position comes an eye for a stride. Some people say 'see a stride' or 'look for a stride'. The Americans call it 'timing', but I use the expression 'pick up a stride'.

Diagram 12. In the dressage position, the balanced rider has a straight, perpendicular line from the ear through the shoulder, hip and heel. Once the rider adopts the jumping position, the line goes through the shoulder, knee and toe, irrespective of how short the stirrups may be. Should the lower leg be pushed further forward, the rider has to stretch and straighten his arms more and lower his shoulders in order to maintain balance.

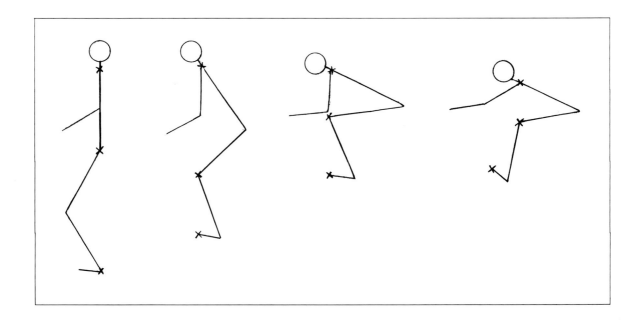

20. A classically perfect show-jumping position – heels down, head up, not collapsing over the horse's neck and allowing the necessary freedom with the rein.

21. Two contrasting styles over the same corner fence. *Left*: Ian Stark with Glenburnie throwing an impressive, powerful jump. Note how the forelegs are tucked up and how high the shoulder has lifted. This picture demonstrates what made him such a good horse. Ian has lost the security of his lower leg and allowed it to drift back – even the great riders have flaws! – but he has resumed the correct position over the top of the fence and would be in a position to be in perfect balance on landing. *Right*: This is a long, flat jump, showing a safe enough technique but suggesting a lack of athleticism. The rider has lost the position of the lower leg and generally appears rather loose in the saddle. Ian seems secure and has merely pivoted on his knee.

22. Note Mark Todd's perfect position throughout (*left*). He is in balance with his horse – weight firmly in the heel, even contact with the horse's mouth, head up, riding forward yet without getting in front of his horse. See how, in the second picture, the lower leg is bracing the drop, and note also the minimum upper-body movement, both of which assist his perfect balance. Notice that the horse has dropped a leg in the first picture, making it all the more important that the rider has a secure position.

Compare the difference in balance between this rider (*above*) and Mark Todd, especially in the second picture, where he is in front of the movement.

23. Different pictures of the same fence showing individual styles. *Top*: A very good picture – secure lower leg, seat low, head up, shoulders not collapsed over the horse's neck and the reins slipped, giving total freedom to the horse. *Bottom*: The rider is pivoting on the knee and as a result of the lack of leg security the shoulders have come too far forward – compare with the top picture. *Top right*: An exaggerated defensive seat. This is not a drop fence, so this is unnecessary. A lack of security of the lower leg with the weight not truly in the heel has made this

rider take a more defensive action – it could be that the horse was hesitant about jumping the fence. *Bottom*: A perfect position on landing – heel down, weight truly on the stirrup, head and shoulders up with freedom for the horse's head and neck. A good safety position should something go wrong – compare this with less secure seats. A lovely picture of balance and harmony.

Worrying whether you are going to meet a fence 'right' tends to dominate the minds of the majority of riders as they make an approach to a fence. With this anxiety comes tension which travels down the arms, down the reins and ends up as restriction at the horse's mouth. In turn, the horse stops going forward and the rider then panics and sends the horse fast, long and flat (on his forehand) into the fence. George Morris, the great American trainer, says that the greatest enemy to a rider's eye is his arm. I would add elbow too, for a stiff elbow has the same effect. The rider who has never heard the expression 'look for a stride' and jumps from blissful ignorance often gives his horse the best chance of jumping. By not interfering at all, the horse is able to keep coming forward and this, coupled with balance, therefore allows him to adjust his stride as necessary. If you think about it, the most you can be wrong is half a stride. This is not a huge distance – six feet. For the horse to shorten his stride by six feet is hardly difficult – after all, that is what we train him to do when doing flat work. However, it is difficult for the horse to shorten his stride if the rider has sent him on a long stride and onto his forehand. The moment the rider commits the horse to taking long steps, it is almost impossible for the horse to shorten them again. The change of balance is too difficult. However, if the rider approaches all the fences with rhythm, balance and the necessary impulsion (the horse will have to be straight if he is to be balanced), he will then find that he will meet the fence on a suitable stride. The horse will be in a position to help make any adjustments, and the whole operation will appear smooth and easy.

The knack in being able to jump effortlessly is to have a well-schooled, obedient horse which can canter in a balanced and rhythmical way. Your job then as a rider is to maintain this balanced canter all the way to the moment the horse takes off. The majority of riders think that they *must* do something and consequently over-ride. Years ago, when I used to bring on some young horses for him, Malcolm Pyrah said something to me which has helped me more than anything else. He had asked me to ride a strange horse to show it off to him. The usual anxiety crept in, and the arms obviously tightened . . . Malcolm said: 'But Jane, you're altering before you see you're wrong.' Well, how true that was and how true it is of many riders. They alter to find a stride rather than 'picking up a stride'. If you can only convince yourself that there is *always* a stride – perhaps if you are jumping 5 foot you need to be more precise, but the most an event rider has to jump is 3 foot 11 inches (unless it is a brush fence). Four foot is forgiving and does not require a precise take-off point. If only we trusted our horses more. . . . They really are better with us sitting still! The rider's job is to create the necessary pace, which must be in rhythm and balanced. Apart from maintaining the impulsion and allowing the horse to carry himself without restriction, we should keep the leg closed and *keep still.* On no account should

24. Two very stylish pictures of Richard Dunwoody jumping the last on Desert Orchid at Cheltenham upsides Norton's Coin. Note Dunwoody's correct position, despite the horse being flat out and under pressure. He is in perfect balance.

be patient without being totally passive. Our legs must ensure that the motor keeps working *all* the way to the point of take-off.

Try jumping small fences, allowing the horse to jump the fence and not 'jumping' it yourself. The horse must jump up from underneath you. You must not 'lift' him over with your hands or your body. Study the National Hunt jockeys. You will see them sitting perfectly still with the minimum movement even over the fences. At that speed, any change of balance is a potential disaster, as most embryo jockeys have learnt to their cost. Watch top jockeys on novice hurdlers and see how quickly they switch to getting in behind their horse the moment they feel the horse hesitate in its stride. Watch your horse loose jump if you can. It should give you enormous confidence that he does not rely on you and that he can organise himself. The only help he needs from you is for you to provide him with the necessary impulsion (he doesn't know what he is going to be asked to jump, but you do), to arrive straight for the middle and help him maintain his rhythm and balance. You will then start to feel rhythm and balance and realise that you do not need to over-shorten the horse's stride to put him spot-on for take-off. If you dominate your horse completely, he will soon start to rely on you totally. The one day you 'miss', the horse will be at a loss to help, so reliant has he become on your helping him. In eventing, when the ground is undulating or when water is involved, it is impossible to 'organise' a horse's stride because ups and downs and water affect the length of stride to an unknown great degree. The horse has to learn to look for himself and look after himself and also you. You teach him how to help by training and this means teaching him to keep a rhythm all the way to a fence.

Everybody picks up bad habits and often we are not aware of these as riders. With so much on which to concentrate, we become oblivious to what is going wrong. Someone on the ground is imperative, every so often at least, just to make you aware of any little faults creeping in. There are times, for instance, when a rider is unaware that he is stopping the horse's forward movement on the approach to a fence. He cannot feel how he is either stiffening in his arm or failing to keep riding and as a result feels the need to increase his riding during the final few strides. It is important to keep the leg on strongly by squeezing (the more you squeeze to take-off, the higher the horse will jump), but the horse's balance should not alter. The stride should not become long and flat, which will happen when the rider drives the horse to the fence having lost his impulsion and forward movement.

When, as a teacher, I feel that the rider is sufficiently

experienced and the horse 'knowing' enough, I set them the following exercise (this should only be done with an experienced person on the ground. It is an 'advanced' exercise and not suitable for inexperienced riders or horses.) I build an easy, inviting fence with a good ground-line. I ask the rider to pick up a 'show-jumping' canter (the kind of canter from which, being full of impulsion, the horse can jump out of his rhythm) and ask him to pop over the fence, checking that his turn is correct. The next time, having asked the rider to turn onto the line into the fence and made sure that the horse was straight, I tell the rider to look at me and not take his eyes off me until he has jumped the fence. I stand level with the fence but far enough away that the rider cannot see it out of the corner of his eye! It is always interesting to see how, every time, the horse meets the fence correctly and can jump easily from the rhythm. Without interference from the rider, the horse's task is made simple. This always demonstrates to the rider exactly how much he was interfering on the approach, and gives him an awareness of the moment when he draws back. This sudden understanding of how much even the smallest amount of interference can affect the jump helps the rider enormously. He can then consciously make the effort to keep riding forward – even if making ahalf-halt – all the way to a fence can see that, so long as the horse can keep coming in a rhythm, balanced and with impulsion, he will always arrive at a suitable take-off point. The moment a rider interferes, this ceases to be possible.

My advice to anyone who is having problems jumping is to say: 'Never stop to look for a stride. Just keep coming with arms feeling as if they are full of air, until you see you are wrong without altering the canter – 99 per cent of the time you will be right. On the rare occasions it might be a case of holding to shorten the stride a fraction by closing the hand or encouraging a longer stride – that's all.' It sounds so simple and it is. We make it much more difficult by doing too much, by doing the wrong thing. In order for this way of riding to a fence to work, however, you *must* have a good canter. A good canter has rhythm, balance and impulsion and this is what working on the flat (dressage) is all about. It is not forcing the horse to trot and canter with its nose firmly held in place and the bit wiggling back and forth in its mouth. It is balance and rhythm in all paces with the horse being able to carry himself within a frame when asked. This is the fundamental understanding so vital to any rider who wishes to event. Yes, dressage, show-jumping and cross-country *do* go hand in hand, but the frame of the horse varies. A horse cannot jump from a restricted frame – he must carry himself in balance with a free neck. Watch the top combinations of horse and rider – you can see for yourself then.

Chapter 2

Tack and Equipment

Correct tack and equipment for horse and rider do actually play a part in jumping clear rounds. Unless both horse and rider are comfortable, they cannot concentrate on the job ahead. Instead, their attention is drawn to some discomfort. Apart from comfort, the other reason for having the correct tack is safety. Poor-quality, old or worn equipment is unsafe. It may cause an accident by breaking, or may mean that you have to pull up in a competition. All this sounds rather 'Pony Club' but unfortunately all too often ill-fitting, unsafe tack is in evidence at horse trials, and not just at Novice level.

If in any doubt about suitable tack, or its fitting ask someone experienced, who is likely to be only to happy to help. Never be too proud to ask! All leather must be good quality – cheap, poorly made tack is just not good enough quality to withstand the rigours and strains that jumping would put on it. It is well worth paying more to get the top quality. The leather for the bridle should be thick enough – show-bridle thickness will not stand up to eventing or racing, for example. Danger points for breaking are the cheekpieces and, of course, the reins. Re-rubbered reins should not be used for competition or fast work and reins should certainly not be re-rubbered more than once. The stitch holes weaken the leather under the rubber – a hidden flaw. Billets are not permitted for racing because they are not strong enough and can snap, and one well-known point-to-point yard in the Midlands area will now not even allow billet-ended reins for exercise, having had several snap in recent years. Reins must either have buckles, be stitched or be loop-ended. Buckles are untidy and stitched reins are a nuisance because you cannot change bits, so the best choice are the loop-ended reins.

A martingale or, preferably, breastplate with martingale attachment or breastgirth is a must to hold the saddle in position – particularly if the rider should fall off and the horse gallop off loose, in which case a martingale also helps to keep the reins from getting tangled round the horse's legs. I look upon a martingale as I look upon a seat belt in the car. You hope you will never need it, but it is there if you ever do. A martingale should not be so tight that it comes into effect under normal circumstances, but if the horse should put his head beyond the point of control, it is there as a reminder. A running martingale which is fitted too tightly will aggravate a horse and possibly cause him to throw up his head against it. When the horse feels the action of the running martingale on the bit, it will cause the bit to act on the bars of the mouth. A horse will always go away from discomfort and not yield to it, so instead of the horse lowering his head when he feels the martingale, he will only raise his head higher. Ensure that your martingale is fitted correctly – as a guideline, it should reach up to the horse's throat, but double-check by holding the reins and seeing that it does not come into action unless the horse raises his head too high.

Girths, stirrup leathers and irons are also potential areas for breakages. Girths must be of staunch material – leather is rather unyielding and heavy, although some do have elastic inserts. Double webbing girths with a surcingle are best. (Most surcingles are made with the elastic inset on the strap end, so making a lump under the rider's leg. Try to find one with the elastic on the buckle end, so that it lies under the horse's stomach.) Lampwick is dangerous because it breaks and I do not advise its use at any time. Wide nylon girths are fine for everyday use but spurs can catch in them, so they are not suitable for use in competitions. Stirrup leathers should be of rawhide, which stretches but will not break, and irons should be stainless steel or aluminium for racing. Nickel is a soft metal and therefore bends – the nightmare of any rider is to be dragged with the foot caught in the stirrup. Nickel irons should be thrown away and not even used for hacking out.

The saddle should fit both horse and rider. It must be forward enough cut to allow the rider to shorten his stirrups to steeple-chase length without his knees coming off the front of the saddle. A good saddle can help the position to a very great extent. A badly made saddle, or one that does not suit the conformation of the rider, can put the rider totally out of balance with his horse. A saddle which puts the rider too far back is bad to ride in, as it forces him perpetually out of balance.

The make of saddle is a personal choice, but when choosing one to ride in cross-country, make sure that you can slide your seat far enough back over a drop fence so that the cantle does not hit you from behind and tip you off (it has happened to me!).

When riding at top level, it is advisable to have two jumping saddles – one for cross-country and one for show-jumping. The cross-country saddle gives you the flexibility to slide back in the seat and ride short. The show-jumping saddle will not need to offer that facility because the rider's seat will never need to lower onto the saddle when jumping. Sometimes when riding cross-country you need to help the horse to keep his hindquarters low – over a drop fence, for example – and by sitting with the seat further back you can influence this. In show-jumping, the horse needs to be encouraged to bring his hindquarters up high over each fence to ensure that he clears the fence behind.

The bit is, again, a matter of choice and what suits your horse. It may be a matter of trial and error to find the bit that your horse goes best in, but correct training should prevent the horse becoming over-strong or resistant. It is always difficult to find a compromise between a horse being keen and being so strong that you cannot control him. A horse that never takes hold is not an easy ride, but similarly an over-strong horse will be a slow horse cross-country because you do not have control at your fingertips. It takes a long time to pull up a very strong horse and valuable time is then wasted. An obedient horse will pull up on request and minimum time is taken. From a snaffle or French link (with two joints in the middle), there are literally hundreds of different kinds of bit to try. A Dr Bristol works well on some horses but may prove too strong for others. The Continental gag has recently become popular, offering a choice of positions for the rein which give more or less control. An ordinary gag never gives a true direct contact, but it is effective for some horses. A roller snaffle, or Magenis, offers another variation for a horse who is difficult to turn. Vulcanite pelhams are mild yet effective, although some horses tend to lean on them and be difficult to turn. It really is a question of trial and error and you might have to keep changing the bit once the horse becomes immune to a particular one. In any case, while a stronger bit may be needed in order to improve control, schooling for obedience is the bottom line in most cases.

The type of noseband depends on what the horse goes best in. A cavesson noseband, simply fitted, may not be enough, in which case a flash noseband provides additional control by the second strap. A grakle noseband has a pressure point where the two straps cross and can be more effective. A drop noseband can interfere with the bit and make some horses resist, whereas others respond well. A Kineton noseband puts a lot of pressure on the nose and will usually anchor the strongest horse. The only important point is that the noseband must fit correctly. All too often one witnesses grakles, flashes or drop nosebands which are so low that they interfere with the horse's breathing.

The legs, front in particular, should always be protected against self-inflicted injuries. A blow on the tendon can cause as much injury as a strain. The effect is the same – damage to the tendon and a long lay-off. Bandages or boots will only give minimum support and are really only useful as protection against the horse striking into himself. A well-fitting boot is far easier to put on and gives as much protection, if not more, as bandages. Bandages are difficult to put on correctly and can cause damage if too tight. If too loose, they can slip and come undone, so they really are a specialist piece of equipment to put on.

For show-jumping, (open-fronted) tendon boots give protection to the all-important tendons, but make the horse aware if he should hit a pole. They are not suitable for cross-country, where protection needs to be given to the shins in case the horse hits a solid fence. The shins of the hind legs need similar protection for cross-country. In show-jumping, the only boot which may be necessary behind is a fetlock protection against brushing.

Overreach boots are never used for racing and I never used them for cross-country for all the years I was competing at Advanced level, none of my horses ever suffering a serious overreach. They can cause problems if the horse treads on them in deep going, making him stumble. They often turn over in water, which renders them useless anyway. They are a matter of choice, but do make sure that if you do use them they are not too big. They are less likely to cause a problem in the show-jumping ring because the horse will not be galloping through mud or water and at least there they can't do any harm unless they are too big or too tight.

Make sure that all tack is securely fastened with keepers and runners in place. A flapping cheekpiece, for example, can soon distract a horse and annoy him (and you!). Try to use your competition tack for serious schooling sessions at home so that you are conversant with its fitting. Nerves at a competition do not go with deciding how to fit something for the first time! I advise making a note of the fitting of all tack so that there can be no last-minute panic.

A good, natural fibre numnah which spreads the pressure (such as a Poly Pad) is essential. Nylon numnahs slip and cause excess sweating. Cotton or sheepskin are best, although the best quality mock sheepskin ones are good. The most important point is that the numnah does not slip or drop down to press on the horse's spine or withers. It needs to be sufficiently thick to give

25. Horse and rider correctly dressed for cross-country competition.

Rider

Crash cap with silk at correct angle for good vision

Body protector

Hunting tie properly tied; stock pins removed

Long-sleeved jumper

Non-slip gloves with or without fingers

Whip – not exceeding 75cms in length. Elastic bands wrapped round handle for grip

Spurs – not exceeding 3.5cms in length, blunt and shank downwards

Buff breeches

Leather riding boots

For schooling, everything should be the same but chaps over suitable trousers or jodphurs and jodphur boots are acceptable.

Horse

Correctly fitted bridle of good quality leather

Loop-ended reins, rubber-covered

Breastplate (or breastgirth)

Martingale

Jumping saddle with numnah, rawhide stirrup leathers and stainless steel irons the right size

Double webbing girths with surcingle with elastic on the buckle end

Tendon boots or correctly applied bandages in front, brushing boots behind

Overreach boots (optional)

Grease on forearms, shins, stifle should only be necessary for Advanced classes

Mane should be plaited or pulled quite short to ease altering of reins

26. Horse and rider incorrectly dressed for cross-country competition.

Rider

Badly fitted crash cap – silk too low – straps too loose

Ill-fitting body protector

No hunting tie (or ready-tied one with stock pins not removed)

Earrings

Leather gloves, gloves without grip or no gloves

Short-sleeved shirt or jumper

Whip too long, no grip on handle, hand through handle, stuck in boot

Spurs too long and upside-down

White breeches on female competitors (not important from safety angle but in rule book as incorrect dress)

Rubber riding boots or half-sole on leather boot, coming detached

Additional incorrect dress for schooling would be tee-shirt, trainers, no crash cap and no body protector

Horse

Ill-fitting cheap and poor quality leather bridle

Leather reins; continental jumping reins; restitched rubber reins; worn reins

No breastplate or breastgirth to keep saddle in place

No martingale

Unsuitable saddle for jumping

Unsafe girth with no surcingle

Nickel irons and not rawhide leathers

Unsuitable slippery nylon numnah (or no numnah)

Badly applied bandages (or no protection at all)

No boots behind

Additional faults would be:

Overreach boots too big

Long, unkempt mane, making it difficult for rider to alter reins maximum comfort, but not too bulky. Although it is a good thing to have a 'best' numnah, do try it out at home a few times to check that it is suitable.

The rider's competition needs are the 'uniform' as set down in the rule books. It is schooling sessions which tend to be rather neglected. Always wear a crash cap and back protector when cross-country schooling. Uncomfortable they may be, but it is far more uncomfortable to be injured through not wearing them. Never ride in unsuitable footwear – anyone who has been dragged will vouch for that. It is still possible to get dragged in correct footwear, so do not aggravate your chances of this nightmare. I always shudder when I see bare arms cross-country. Having severely skinned my elbow in a fall, I know how *very* sore it can be. I therefore recommend long sleeves however hot it is.

Jodphurs, jeans, long boots or chaps? Again, a matter of choice. As long as you can ride efficiently, it is unimportant. I would advise wearing 'competition' boots on several home occasions because riding in chaps and jodphur boots is very different from riding in long boots. Similarly, use spurs and carry a whip when schooling cross-country.

It always amazes me how the majority of event riders can see where they are going when they wear the silks on their crash caps so low. It is unnecessary for the peak to be at the same angle as a jockey's, but when you are in the forward position it is very difficult to see when the brim is so low. Maybe this is why event riders sit so upright when riding the steeplechase . . .

I know that if I am uncomfortable, feeling bulky in too many clothes or riding on a saddle which does not fit me, I never ride as well as I do when everything is right. As a result, this chapter is as much about jumping clear rounds as the other chapters. Ill-fitting clothes or tack may not directly be responsible for faults jumping, but they are an influence which must be considered.

Chapter 3

The Show-Jumping Course

The show-jumping phase tends to be the *bête noire* of the average event rider. This dismal view of show-jumping stems from lack of training of both horse and rider and also lack of practical experience. From this comes a lack of confidence. To be a proficient event rider, it is vital to practise and perfect the art of jumping a course of at least four-foot fences. Unless horse and rider can jump a course in rhythm and balance, then they should not even contemplate setting off on a cross-country course of similar standard. Alas, how often does one see a disastrous show-jumping round, followed by a hairy – albeit without penalties – cross-country display. A clear round here is obtained with luck and on a wing and a prayer. Luck will only hold out for so long – eventually problems will occur.

Apart from a good show-jumping round being proof of correct training, it is also important if you want to win. Show-jumping penalties are costly. Clear rounds do not just 'happen'. They require planning and concentration. This starts when walking and assessing the course. It is important to walk the show-jumping course as carefully as the cross-country. Admittedly, the terrain in the show-jumping arena will not be as varied as on the cross-country, but the turns, distances and any slight gradients must be observed and noted. If all hinges on a clear round, such as at a major competition, or if the track is big or complicated, it is wise to walk the course at least twice. A small, straightforward track will be far more forgiving than a difficult one, when any mistake of presentation at a fence will be costly in faults.

Take stock of the general impression of the course. Is it well-built and imposing, or is it flimsy with little to set up the horse? Is it twisty or flowing? How many related distances, combinations and doubles are there? Are there any difficult turns? All these questions reveal the pattern of the course and will influence how you ride it. At the same time you have to assess the suitability of the course to your own horse. Only you know whether your horse is spooky and will be worried by a brightly coloured filler, whether you need to have more impulsion than normal to get round without a refusal, or whether your horse is bold and a little

71

27. A well-dressed show-jumping course offers a much more inviting track to jump than a flimsy one. Fillers, flowers and brightly coloured poles give the horse something to look at. With a young, spooky horse, this may mean that the rider has to be much more positive and determined in his riding to avoid a refusal. For an experienced horse who can be a little casual or over-keen, a well-built course is preferable by far. As a horse backs off, provided that the rider keeps the impulsion, it has the effect of bringing the hocks underneath the horse and lightening the forehand. The most common problem a rider has when riding an experienced horse over a set of inspiring looking fences is that the horse runs through his hand on the approach to a fence. As a result, the horse does not alter his balance onto his hindquarters but finds the balance in his rider's hand. No balance means no rhythm, so the horse loses the power to lengthen and shorten his stride if necessary. By backing off the imposing looking fences, the horse is automatically setting himself up and the rider merely has to 'keep coming' for the fences to be met on easy strides.

A flimsy course gives the horse nothing to look at or respect. There is nothing to set him up and he is encouraged to become careless and lacking in effort. This applies to a cross-country course too. A big, well-built course may appear daunting on a walk-round, but horses will respect the fences and set themselves up. An innocent, flimsy rail will prove far more difficult to jump than a big, solid-looking obstacle and when walking any course a rider must never be dismissive of some apparently straightforward, small, uncomplicated fence. This is the type that often proves to be a real 'trip-up' obstacle, catching the unwary. The less imposing an obstacle, the more respectful you have to be as a rider, because your horse will not be. A simple upright fence with poles is the fence that most horses will kick out without a care, whereas a terrifyingly bright parallel, decked with flowers and bushes, is often jumped with feet to spare.

careless, so will jump better over a more imposing track. As you walk round, ask yourself these questions because the answers will help you decide on how to set about jumping round clear. Take careful note of the start and finish and familiarise yourself with the bell or buzzer used to start competitors. Although the first fence will be the smallest and most straightforward on the course, it often catches out the more novicey horse or rider (as well as an experienced combination on the odd occasion!). Its siting is influential; if built away from home or the collecting ring, there will be more chance of a horse stopping than if built towards home. You must know your horse's character and whether he automatically speeds up when turned towards home or other horses. At least if you expect a certain reaction, you will not be caught out by being taken by surprise.

A golden rule when jumping any fence is that you must be straight. Turns into fences or lines of fences are therefore of paramount importance. If you allow yourself to fall into the bad habit of looking down over fences as you jump them, riding a course and finding good lines will prove to be very difficult. Let your eyes find the lines, so look up and ahead and do not be afraid to turn your head. So many people ride as if their head and neck were solidly joined to their body!

28. A turn into a fence in the show-jumping arena. The horse is in good balance and the rider is in a good position for re-balancing his horse on the corner.

29. The horse is resisting the rider's hand on the turn and is lacking balance.

Walk all related distances and decide whether they will ride easily for your horse. It is only by jumping regularly round courses of fences that you will recognise a pattern of related distances relative to your horse. If you limit the number of rounds you do to the number of horse trials you enter, then you will seriously lack the necessary show-jumping experience. To learn from experience, it is worthwhile writing down the distances you walk, whether it is vertical to a spread or *vice versa*, and how it rode. In this way, you will soon build up a pattern. Try out these distances at home – never forget that clear rounds are not just good luck. They represent hours of hard work and background training of both horse *and* rider.

Be observant about lines of fences. A wide spread followed by an upright will catch many horses. The spread will encourage a big flat jump, probably followed by an unbalanced landing, and the vertical demands a balanced jump off the hocks. The horse will take time to recover his balance after the spread and, unless quickly rebalanced, the vertical will be influential. A true parallel requires more accuracy than an ascending spread and demands greater balance and rhythm. If there is an alternating parallel (one side higher than the other, like a wide cross-pole) then note your line – slightly off-centre with the front pole lower than the back one. Take note of any turn into it because any inaccuracy on the turn will affect the precise line necessary for this type of fence. Having walked the course, try to allow time to watch a few competitors with critical appreciation, and avoid falling into the traps of mistakes you witness.

Watching other competitors can be useful. On the other hand, it may give a false impression of the course. It is important not to become demoralised by seeing horse after horse making mistakes. Try to assess the experience and level of training of the horses and riders before deciding that the course is impossibly difficult. Take note of any fence which horses are tending to hit and try to decide why. Is it a related distance? Does the ground alter? Is it away from home? Is the turn difficult? Is it that horses are becoming unbalanced? Having decided the reason for the problem, work out how you will try to ensure that your horse has the best possible chance of jumping without fault. In related distances, only take note of how the distances are riding if you can see that the horse you are watching is similar to your own. There is little point in watching a short-striding horse struggle to make a distance – and deciding that the distance must be long – if your horse is long-striding. Try to watch a horse with a similar stride and way of going to your own before deciding that the distance will not ride as walked.

Show-jumping is technical, and the higher the standard, the more technical it becomes. Flowing round as if on a cross-country course rarely works. With the standard improving all the time, the various aspects of eventing have become more difficult. There is a limit to how demanding the cross-country and dressage can be, so it is the show-jumping which has had to be made more influential. To my mind, this is no bad thing. Show-jumping is a test of obedience of the horse, in the same way that dressage is. Show-jumping is often 'poo-pooed' by those who find it difficult. These people often spend hours working at their dressage, but neglect the all-important aspect of jumping training. A clear round in the show-jumping is proof of correct training in the same way that a low dressage mark is the sign of a well-trained horse on the flat. All this schooling should then be put into practice at speed in the cross-country phase. An uneducated horse and rider going cross-country becomes a potential disaster. A horse which can jump a disciplined show-jumping round will be able to reproduce the same cross-country. The two go hand-in-hand.

Take careful note of the time allowed. Time faults can be costly, particularly in a three-day event, and many an event has been won or lost on a time fault. If the time is riding tight, work out how you are going to make up time. Cutting corners or increasing the pace round long turns is normally sufficient. Obviously you want to avoid having to increase the pace into the fences themselves. Your horse must be obedient in changing pace – this is where all your long hours of schooling come into practice – and should be able to change from a slow canter to a fast one and back again without resistance. Resistance will lead to fences being knocked down. Resistance indicates a lack of balance and will give a horse little chance of jumping well. Making up time in the show-jumping is similar to cross-country riding. Jump each fence correctly with rhythm and balance, then as soon as you have landed, pick up an increased pace, then rebalance and readjust the pace in time for the next fence. The time for the show-jumping at a three-day event is tight, so you should practise being able to increase the pace at shows throughout the year. Jumping jump-off rounds gives plenty of practice for this – but you have to show-jump often enough to get into enough jumps-off for practice!

The warming-up period is crucial for riding clear rounds. Too much work in the collecting ring and the horse will be dull and liable to rub a pole through being flat and lacking sparkle. Not enough work will mean that the horse is too exuberant and probably lacking concentration as a result. Again, it is practice and knowing your horse which will tell you the ideal length of time. At a one-day event, the horse will have already had a minimum of, say, threequarters of an hour's work (probably more!) so he should only require about twenty minutes' warm-up prior to jumping in the ring.

Working-in for jumping follows the same principles as for dressage. You are aiming for a supple, obedient horse who is willing to carry out your demands without resistance. The difference lies in the outline of the horse and his approach to his work. In dressage, you want your horse to await every command and remain in a frame throughout each movement. He must be attentive to the rider and be totally submissive – see the wording on a dressage sheet regarding the collective marks: submission, attention and obedience, lightness and ease of movement, acceptance of the bridle. For jumping, the horse must be balanced, rhythmical and obedient, but he must be allowed to carry himself in a less restricted outline. His attitude must be focussed rather more on what lies ahead than totally on his rider, so that he is able to assess the situation for himself when he arrives at a fence. This does not mean that he takes matters into his own hands – he must remain obedient to the aids but be less dominated by the rider. His outline should be natural so that he can have free use of his head and neck on the approach, over and on landing over a fence. When riding-in for show-jumping, make sure that you work the horse in his jumping outline and supple him without necessarily being in a frame. When warming-up over the practice fence, it is vital that the horse does not feel restricted. All too often riders tense up in the collecting ring, ending up with a horse cramped into a 'dressage' outline and therefore unable to jump to its best ability.

When warming-up, start with some preliminary trot work, then concentrate on the horse's canter. It is, after all, from canter that the course will be jumped. Endless trotting will be of little benefit. Placing poles are not permitted under FEI or BHS rules (see the BHS *Horse Trials Rule Book*) in conjunction with the practice fence, so no poles can be used in front of a fence. (Make sure you are conversant with the rules of permitted fences and take note of the flagging of the practice fences.) A cross-pole is best to commence the jumping warm-up. This can be approached in trot for the horse to 'pop' over, just to loosen up. The cross ensures that the horse jumps straight over the middle of the fence. This should be done a couple of times to get the horse and rider into 'jumping mode'. With the excitement of a competition, horses sometimes lose concentration over a tiny fence, so make sure that you are prepared for any unexpected take-off – a jab in the mouth is something a horse will not forget and a trauma which must be avoided at all costs. If you should get left behind, slip your reins, but do not punish the horse in the mouth, even if you think he was silly to take off where he did.

From the cross-pole, you can progress to a small upright in canter. A ground pole at the base of the wing feet will help to make the upright more inviting. Once the horse has jumped an upright a few times (raise it a little to just below maximum permitted height) you should then move to a spread fence. To give horse and rider confidence, a cross-pole in front offers an inviting fence to jump first. Change it then to a slightly ascending spread and then to a parallel. Make sure that the ground rail is immediately underneath the front rail for this, so encouraging the horse to throw a good, athletic jump. A ground rail at the feet of the wings will encourage a flat jump over a spread. Always bear in mind the purpose of the practice fences. You are preparing your horse to be as athletic as possible and the aim in the practice ring is to make him jump by using himself and to make an effort. If all the practice fences you jump are ones which require no effort on the horse's part, he will be unprepared to make an effort in the ring when faced with a square parallel, for example.

Having opened the horse out over a spread, return to the upright fence to 'get him back in the air' again. Use the ground pole to help him back off if necessary. Some horses benefit from jumping an upright with the pole directly beneath the top rail.

The practice arena tends to be one of the most revealing places, showing up those who have a plan of what they are doing, as opposed to those who jump in a haphazard fashion, with no real idea of what they are working towards.

For horse trials, it is against the rules to jump higher than the maximum height of the fences in the ring. Make sure that you do jump a parallel of that height so that it does not come as a shock when the horse is faced with a maximum-sized fence in the ring. The number of times you jump a particular fence depends upon how the horse is jumping and the experience of both horse and rider. A less experienced combination will probably need more jumping outside the ring to build up confidence and dispel any nerves or tension. A more demanding course will need more thorough warming-up and athletic jumping than a small track. It should be common-sense how much you jump before going into the ring – not enough and the horse may be unprepared, too much and he will be jaded and you will have left your clear round in the collecting ring.

Everybody gets nervous to various degrees when competing. The level of nerves depends on the experience of the rider, the horse he is riding and the importance of the occasion. Some riders cope better with nerves than others. In some, it makes them ride better; others go to pieces. The more disciplined and practised the horse and rider, the less influential these nerves will be. This is another reason why it is *vital* to have as much show-jumping practice as possible to try to alleviate tension and nerves from the worry of it being difficult. The more you jump, the less difficult it will become. The show-jumping phase will be just another round and the rider can relax in himself and ride helpfully rather than hindering his horse. Nerves and tension in the show-jumping, as in anything else, create a vicious circle. The more tension there is, the more likelihood there is of mistakes being made. It is not a coincidence that the top riders make it look so easy and relaxed – this is the attitude that must be adopted. A relaxed yet positive attitude from the rider will give the horse every chance to relax himself and concentrate. A rider who grabs at his horse, altering the rhythm and firing the horse into each fence in his anxiety to get over, gives his horse no help at all. A good mental approach is so important and only comes with practice and experience.

You have to know what your horse needs and you should have learnt this through jumping at home and from a pattern of warming-up you have used at jumping shows. It is not always easy to time finishing your practice jump with your turn to enter the ring. It is often beneficial to jump another fence before you go into the ring if you have been walking for some time. Waiting is always an anxious moment, and jumping another fence after a long wait releases tension. I know from experience that there are moments when you are feeling particularly nervous when you can't imagine what it is like to jump a fence. You almost think you have forgotten how! Your legs feel like jelly and you feel totally pathetic. The best way to get rid of this feeling is to 'get on with it'. So, if you begin to feel like that while you wait your turn, make sure you pop another fence and then try to go straight into the ring. You and your horse must not 'go off the boil' but be mentally and physically prepared for action. All too often, a novice rider will arrive at the first fence with his horse totally unprepared and half-asleep. They then grind to a halt at the first fence. Often, having pulled themselves together, they then go on to jump a clear round! The horse must be aware of what he is going to do. Conversely, the horse should not be worked into a frenzy like a pony at the start of a gymkhana game! The balance must be found between over- and under-riding – again, practice makes perfect.

Warming-up for the show-jumping phase of a three-day event requires careful planning. The horse is liable to be stiff and weary. His energy levels will be limited yet he must be thoroughly loosened up and suppled before he can be expected to jump. He will have had quite some time walking in the morning for the veterinary inspection but unless the jumping follows on immediately afterwards, this will be of little benefit. It is important to understand that riding a horse on the third day of a three-day event is not like riding the horse you know. He may be slow to respond, heavy and stiff. The fitter the horse and the less punishing the cross-country, the less evident this will be. Be prepared for a change, though, and realise that your help will be needed. This means sitting lightly in the saddle and not expecting too much from the horse. His canter may lack spring and he may jump in a laboured fashion. Your job is to concentrate on keeping the balance and rhythm, and ensuring that you create enough impulsion. Riding a tired horse is rather like driving a car with a flat tyre which is running out of petrol!

After some suppling work on the flat, you should pop your horse over a couple of small fences, just to get a feel for how he is jumping. Find out how many competitors there are before you and try to time your jumping so that you do not have to hang around for too long after your jumping practice. Remember that you are not going to improve your horse's jump at this stage. It is a case of trying to make him use himself, yet also preserving energy. Do not canter round for ages prior to jumping or between jumps. Jump the practice fence and then walk while it is altered. You can follow the one-day event pattern of cross-pole from trot, small vertical from canter, bigger vertical, then to an ascending spread, followed by a true parallel building up to maximum height and width; then back to the vertical. Do not over-jump – it is the easiest mistake to make. Ensure that the horse does make some effort and that you do not fall into the trap of approaching on long strides, which is the tendency when riding a tired horse. He will be erring on the long side and it will require hard work from the rider to keep him together. (It is not a valid excuse to say: 'Ah well, we were doing cross-country yesterday.') Do not expect the horse to be able to work for long – keep the jumping to a minimum. If you do find you have longer to wait than you anticipated, go and jump one more fence. Resist the temptation to jump more than once, even if the horse knocks it down. If he knocks it hard enough, it might be the reminder he needs!

The pressure on the show-jumping day of a three-day event is enormous. Make sure that you know the course. Sit down quietly somewhere and go through it in your mind. Ride every turn and every fence. Many a famous rider has taken the wrong course – it is so easy to do when you are concentrating hard on other things.

We tend to feel cold when we are tired. Horses are the same, so make sure that you keep a rug thrown over your horse's back when he is not working. Cold muscles are stiff, so you need to keep the muscles as warm as possible. Keep the horse gently on the move – again, muscles must not be allowed to stiffen up. There is so much more to jumping a clear round than meets the eye; and how expensive a fault can be.

Practice fence procedure

The practice arena can be an over-crowded, frustrating area. There you are, knowing exactly what you want to do and where you want to go and you find you are bumped, headed for, cut across and generally aggravated by fellow competitors. The lower the level, the more apparent this may be and all the more disruptive because you are on a young, skittish horse which shies and jumps sideways when other horses come near.

We all tend to think that the practice arena is for our benefit only. Alas, it is not. Everyone, whatever standard, has as much right to work there and jump the practice fence as you. Apart from the fact that it is ill-mannered to curse and swear at other competitors, it is unlikely to put you in the frame of mind necessary for jumping a clear round. If you become angry and frustrated, your horse will soon pick up the vibes and become tense himself. This will further irritate you and a vicious circle commences.

Bear in mind that most riders are paralysed with nerves in the collecting ring. Their limbs refuse to work and their brain goes on strike. Their reactions become slow and they are probably so engrossed in what they are doing that they scarcely notice other horses and riders. In their state of nerves they become oblivious to everything else. Have sympathy, therefore. Do not leave your warming-up to the last minute so that there is no time to wait your turn – it is not anyone else's fault if you are late, so do not take it out on nervous fellow competitors. That is just what they do not need!

Jumping the practice fence can be like pulling out onto a busy road. You have to be ready and quick to take your chance. Try not to canter endless circles as you wait – you will lose your good canter. Keep your wits about you and slot in. It may be that you have to pick up a canter and turn to the fence immediately. Try doing this at home. Do not feel you need to canter half way round the school before you are ready to jump. This is a common fault. Riders feel they must canter a circle and it takes them ages to become mentally prepared to jump. At home, pretend you are in the collecting ring – if possible have a group jumping session – and practise going straight into canter from walk, turning and jumping a fence. Perfecting this will help enormously when working in a collecting ring with minimum room for manoeuvre and will prevent you becoming hot and bothered when you should be cool, calm and collected.

Show-jumping fences

Although the approach for any fence is basically the same, the different types of obstacle found in the show-jumping ring do require slightly individual treatment.

General rules for jumping any type of fence are: make sure that your line of approach is straight for the centre of the fence (other than in exceptional circumstances) and make sure that the horse is going forward in balance, that there is enough impulsion maintained to jump individual fences and that the horse maintains rhythm all the way to take-off.

● *Ascending spread*
This is an oxer where the front rail is lower than the back rail. It is the easiest fence to jump. The spread gives the fence an imposing nature and something definite for the horse to look at and judge his take-off point from. As the front rail is lower, fewer demands are placed on the horse's front-leg technique and he does not have to be so quick in front. He will size up the back pole as the highest point and, in aiming to clear that, will normally clear the lower front pole. The hind legs should follow the shape of the bascule, so unless the horse hollows over the fence, he should clear the back pole with his hind legs too. On the approach, ensure that there is enough impulsion for the height and width of the fence.

● *Parallel or square oxer*
The front and back poles are the same height, so placing a demand on the horse's jumping technique as well as his ability and power. He must be quick in front and also be able to follow the jump through by 'opening out' behind to avoid hitting the back rail. A parallel is the greatest test of a horse's scope and jumping ability. It requires maximum balance and rhythm and, depending on the size of the fence, impulsion. It requires an accurate jump – if the horse stands off too far, he will probably flatten and catch the front pole behind. If he gets in too deep, he will either catch the front pole with his front legs or go up and down and land on the back pole. The range of take-off points is not as great as for an ascending spread, so there is less margin for error.

● *Triple bar*

This is a staircase fence with poles at progressively higher settings. It is an inviting fence to jump, with no premium put on front-leg technique apart from the ability to clear the highest rail. It does require maximum impulsion and a slight increase in pace may even be necessary if the spread is wide. The rider must be careful not to allow the horse to lengthen and fall onto his forehand if the pace is increased, and any increase must not be left until the last few strides. It must be well established on the approach. Normally when looking at a fence you study the front pole. In fact it is best to look at the middle pole in a triple bar, because there will be less chance of you asking the horse to stand off too far, which is the risk from judging the front pole. If the horse lacks impulsion, he will struggle to make the width and will catch the top rail, or even try to 'paddle' through the fence. Either will give the horse an uncomfortable feeling and may affect his confidence at this type of fence for the future.

Be aware that a filler as part of the front rail will make the fence more imposing for a young horse, so be ready to create a little more impulsion, ensuring you maintain this and the rhythm all the way to the fence to counteract any hesitation on the horse's part.

● *Uprights*

An upright fence may be constructed from a variety of materials such as poles, planks, a gate or a wall. An upright is all on the same plane, thus making the take-off point difficult for the horse to judge. Being a technically difficult fence, a premium is placed on balance and rhythm. Any flaw here will be rewarded by a knock-down. All riders know that uprights claim more victims than spread fences and tend to try too hard to clear them. In their efforts to try to make the horse jump higher, they often 'lift' the horse either with their hands or with their bodies. This has the effect of making the horse either hollow over the fence or lose his balance at take-off and therefore not jump high enough. The rider should concentrate on making the rhythm and balance perfect and sitting absolutely still until the horse takes off. At the point of take-off the rider should make minimum movement with his body – always try to remember that it is the *horse* that jumps the fence, not the rider.

● *Stiles*

A stile is any narrow fence, although traditionally an upright made with white poles and a mock foot support. It is not an easy fence. Its narrowness is distracting for the horse and also invites a run-out. In his lack of concentration and respect for the fence, the horse can appear to be careless.

A stile is a true test of a horse's obedience and training. A young horse will find this type of fence difficult becase he is not strictly between his rider's hand and leg, so he may wander off a straight line from lack of balance. It is vital that the line of approach is 100 per cent straight and that the horse is in perfect rhythm and balance. He must be given plenty of time to assess the situation and see his way through the fence. If taken by surprise, the horse will be given little chance to clear the fence. Any hesitation will cause loss of forward movement which in turn creates loss of rhythm and impulsion. It is a temptation for the rider to 'lift' the horse but this is as detrimental here as for any fence. The contact should be kept until take-off – if the horse is dropped at such a fence, it is an invitation to run out. The more worried a rider is about a particular sort of fence, the more likely the horse is to hit it. By worrying, the rider becomes tense. Tension stops forward movement, affects the balance and rhythm and the horse has little opportunity to jump. Try to treat even the most tricky fence in the same way, being positive on the approach and establishing the necessary balance and rhythm in plenty of time.

● *Alternating spread/St Andrew's Cross*
Here you should deviate from the rule of always jumping every fence in the middle. The fence is a spread cross-pole and you should aim to jump it slightly to one side, thus making it an ascending spread as opposed to a true parallel, which it is in the middle. If, for example, the front pole is higher on the left and the back pole higher on the right, you would choose a point slightly right of centre to jump it. If you drift too far right, the back pole would be very high. Horses are more likely to hit fences in front than behind, so by taking a line right of centre (in this instance) although the back rail is gradually becoming higher, the horse should clear it. He will aim to throw a bigger jump to clear the back pole with his forelegs and provided that he does not hollow in the air, the parabola should allow him to clear the back pole behind.

A problem can arise with this type of fence if the horse drifts to one side as he takes off. Bear this in mind when choosing your line. Practise at home to learn the best way for your horse to approach these fences.

● *Doubles, combinations and related distances*
When walking these, it is important that you are consistent with
your own stride length as you pace out distances to measure the
number of strides your horse will take. It takes practice and
experience. When walking any distance, always look down (the
only time you should!). Do not look at the fence ahead because
your eyes will encourage you to alter your step to meet the
distance correctly.

These fences should be easy to jump provided that you meet the
first element with the correct rhythm, balance and impulsion. All
the grid-work practised at home should come into play and the
rider should concentrate on keeping the horse straight and
keeping the rhythm. At the same time, he should think about his
position and forward swing and ensure that he never gets in front
of his horse in his anxiety to jump through the elements. A young
horse may spook at brightly coloured fillers at subsequent
elements. The rider must learn to strike the balance between
under- and over-riding. Over-riding will cause the horse to flatten
and lose balance.

Related distances only cause trouble if the horse lacks impulsion, rhythm or balance and the rider must make sure that the
approach is straight and the horse is prepared well in advance.

These fences are proof of all the training work done at home.
They only cause problems to horses who cannot keep an even
stride and lose balance on landing. In other words, lack of
training will be exposed. The distance between any elements,
whether it be one or five strides, does depend upon how the horse
jumps the first part. The rider must be quick to assess this and be
ready to increase or decrease pace as necessary to make the
appropriate distance. This adjustment is a case of either quickly
sending the horse forward, should he land short over the first
part, or holding to shorten the stride if the horse jumps the first
part very big. Speed of reaction comes from practice and
experience.

● *Water jumps*
If the course contains a water jump, you should decide whether
you will increase pace (approximately half-a-dozen strides at an
increased pace should give enough impetus to clear the spread of
water) and, depending on the type of fence which follows it, how
quickly you will have to re-establish the balance after it. If the
water jump is followed by an upright or true parallel, a premium
will be placed on obedience and control.

Chapter 4

Walking the Cross-Country Course and Warming-up

Walking the course

'Time spent on reconnaissance is seldom wasted.' Never is this saying more appropriate than when applied to walking a cross-country course. The more detailed attention paid to the approach and nature of each fence, the better the chance will be of a trouble-free cross-country round. The more difficult and technical the course, the more attention to detail must be paid. So often a competition is lost due to lack of thought put into how each fence must be ridden. A balance must be found, however, between the over-technical approach when every fence is analysed to such an extent that the rider becomes almost mesmerised with detail and so loses his or her natural flair, and the over-casual approach. This too can lead to problems. Every fence has to be jumped and has its own pitfall and riders have to decide which fences do genuinely warrant lengthy perusal and which are straightforward.

Whatever the course, do not forget that your first impression of every fence as you walk towards it is what the horse will see. The difference is that you are approaching on your feet at a slow pace whereas the horse will be arriving at the fence considerably faster and with less time to assess the situation. Many fences are not what they appear to be from some distance away. There may be a hidden drop or ditch lurking behind the fence. When walking, take careful note of the fences which are not what they seem on initial viewing, because these are the ones which may catch out your horse. On subsequent walks round, you will not have that same first impression because you know what hazard each fence holds, so make sure you concentrate on your first walk round to ensure you do not miss that important aspect of the course. It is interesting to note that courses which vary little from year to year

30. This is what the horse will see as he approaches a fence into darkness. Unless he is given a chance to assess the situation, he will understandably be most reluctant to jump into an apparent void. This rider is riding positively to the fence. From her body position, she has had to stay in behind her horse until he took off to ensure that he jumped into the unwelcoming darkness. She has kept the balance stable and kept the horse off his forehand. Despite the fact that her lower leg has curled back slightly, the position is secure. If a horse is taken by surprise and unprepared for a fence such as this, he has every reason to refuse.

31. A drop fence from the take-off will look innocent. The drop will be hidden on the approach. It is only when you inspect the landing side that you see the hidden hazard. Your horse will not know what is beyond until he comes down to land in the case of a straightforward drop hedge, for example. You must prepare him for the shock and ensure that the balance is correct on the approach – we have all seen the effect when the horse lengthens to a drop, falling onto his forehand in the process. He is so unbalanced on landing that he has little chance of staying on his feet, particularly if the going is deep.

32. A combination fence on the approach can appear to be a complete jumble of poles. It is only as you draw near and examine what is before you that you can disentangle the mass of poles and see a way through. Always remember that first impression – remember that you are approaching at walking pace and have plenty of time to decipher the problem in your mind. The horse will be approaching at a much faster pace and has precious little time to assess what is ahead. How important it is, therefore, for the rider to give him every possible opportunity to see clearly what he has to do. Apart from the distance between elements, for which a galloping stride is unsuitable, a fast approach gives the horse no time to evaluate the various elements. He must be allowed time to see, and brought in on a correct line in good time so that the way through is obvious. It is so unfair on your horse to spring a surprise on him of this nature – an event horse has to be quick-witted even when correctly presented at various obstacles. To present him incorrectly is abusing his trust in you.

often cause significant problems. This is invariably because riders fail to 'see' the problem that is presented to a new horse owing to their own familiarity with the course.

It is essential to have some idea of the route the course takes before you set off to walk round. Always carry a programme with you. The programme should also have a map of the course which may prove invaluable if you are forced to walk the course early in the morning in inclement, foggy weather. Count each fence and check on the programme that you have not missed one out. You can more or less guarantee that at least one competitor is eliminated for missing out a fence during a competition. Check off the fences as you walk them. You can then jot down comments concerning the course, such as landmarks to help find correct lines, the need to avoid bad going or other observations. In the case of a three-day event, this is imperative. I would make comments on trees to line up with on the long approach to a particular fence, or a landmark level with which you start to steady in preparation for a fence – all these things seem obvious at the time of walking but it is so easy to forget the small details, particularly when there is so much else to remember.

On a long course with nearly thirty fences, if you waste time turning into or away from each fence, or start to steady much earlier than necessary because you cannot quite remember where to turn, or where the fence is sited, you could waste as much as half a minute, if not more. A fast time across country does not depend on the speed you jump the fences but on the economy of the route and the rhythm of the round. This means that you must be 100 per cent conversant with the course and know *exactly* when and where to start each approach and the line to be taken to the next fence the moment you land from the previous one.

It is useful to walk a course with someone more experienced than yourself, although you are the one who knows your horse and you should not be swayed by anyone who does not know either you or your horse well. It is necessary to concentrate when walking, so try to prevent the course walk from becoming a social occasion with the latest scandal being discussed. At a one-day event, when there is generally only time to walk the course once, it can be difficult to escape friends, but chatting all the way round is not conducive to concentration.

Ideally the course should be walked more than once. In the case of a three-day event, it should be a minimum of three times. The length and severity of the track determines how often you need to walk it. If you have already ridden a course, it is a definite advantage because it is not until you actually ride it that you become truly familiar with the way it rides. At a one-day event, it is usually impractical from the time point of view to manage to walk a course more than once. You may have time to nip back to a couple of the more tricky fences if you have ample time between phases. If you can walk the course the night before, it is a distinct advantage – unless you then spend all night as a gibbering wreck! On the positive side, you then do at least have time to go over the course in your mind several times and you should also have time to go back and look at some of the fences the next morning.

At a three-day event, the first walk round the course should be your first impression walk when you form a general idea and take note of all the take-offs, landings and the undulations in the terrain. You will have a vague plan of how you will jump most of the fences but should have an open mind until you have studied the fences in more detail. The second walk round is when you should finalise your route, decide the most direct route, look very carefully at the option fences and examine the penalty zones in detail. Have a clear notion in your head of all possible routes and decide on your Plan A, Plan B and what you would do if you had a problem at any element. Work out precisely what you would do if your horse stopped at the first, second or third part. Valuable time is lost if the rider spends time working out which way he must go after a refusal. All this must be crystal clear. Similarly, your second chosen route must be as carefully walked as the first choice. You must decide what factors would make you deviate from your original plan. For example, if you were held up for some time on the course it would be wise to choose an easier option at the next fence. Having stopped, your rhythm will be broken and the horse is likely to have switched off. Trying to jump a very difficult fence before you have got back into the rhythm again is asking for trouble. If the horse is not jumping as fluently or boldly as normal, it would be wise to opt for some easier alternatives. If the horse makes a bad mistake at the fence before a difficult option fence, it could be worth going the longer, less demanding route. If a competitor who has had trouble previously was still negotiating the fence as you approached, it would be too much to expect your horse to concentrate sufficiently to jump a complicated route which demanded full control and accuracy. Experience on the rider's part will enable him to make split-second decisions, but he also needs common-sense linked with clear thinking.

The third walk round a three-day event course is the one you

33. Water throws strong reflections, particularly in the sunshine. When walking slowly towards such a fence, it can be quite dazzling and takes a moment for the eyes to adjust to what is actually there. For a horse, approaching at speed, with no prior knowledge of what lies ahead, it is even more perplexing – sunshine and shadows can play tricks with the eyes – so it is vital that he is allowed to weigh up what he has to do, without being given the option of stopping.

should walk entirely on your own, imagining you are actually riding the course. You should visualise approaching each fence, pretending that you are giving the aids to 'gather' the energy, bouncing the horse into a tricky combination or riding strongly into a daunting obstacle. Imagine how your horse should feel on the approach to each, remember how he felt when the approach was incorrect at times at previous events, and know what you are going to do to improve it quickly. Picture what could go wrong, and picture how it should (and will!) be. Ride the course in your mind and be positive.

If you walk the approach to each fence as if you were riding it, you will find yourself walking briskly and with a purpose. If you saunter towards every fence, it suggests that that is how you will ride them. Do not worry what you look like – you have to be quite potty to event anyway! I could be seen walking towards a fence looking as if I was riding an imaginary hobby horse, clicking and holding imaginary reins – this mental imagery made all the difference to me.

When assessing each fence, it is important that you can see it through your horse's eyes. This is when your first impression of the fence is so useful. Take into account how you see, for example, a table fence and how a horse sees it. You see a table fence as an imposing solid obstacle. For the horse, who only has a relatively thin top-line to see and no ground-line, the fence is very difficult to judge. This is why these sorts of fences cause so many falls – the rider and the horse interpret them in opposite ways. So, try to imagine how your horse will see the fences, not how you see them. Take into account any distractions which may take his eye off the fence itself. This is particularly important with a young horse who does not concentrate easily. When riding at a big event, take into account that there will be a large crowd of people standing round the fences. Make sure that the landmark you use to find your line is a high one – a low one will disappear behind the crowd. Take note of where the crowd is likely to be and decide whether it will then change the whole aspect of the fence. A sea of faces can be intimidating for a horse, particularly one not used to crowds, and will have a 'backing-off' effect.

When walking a three-day event course, try to make one of your trips at approximately the same time of day as when you will ride it. Although walking takes infinitely longer than riding it, you should be given some indication of how sun and shadow may influence particular fences. Shadow can affect fences in different ways. Light through trees can throw a dappling effect on a fence.

34. It is amazing how a fence can change character with the effect of a crowd. With a twisty course where the fence is approached off a turn, such as at Badminton, the fence may disappear altogether until you round the corner and are suddenly presented with it. How vital it is that you know your line precisely and are not reliant on the fence itself to find the line of approach. At a Novice event, this is rarely a problem. It is only at the more major competitions that crowds become a problem. However, even at a small three-day event, the water jump will always attract a mass of spectators and the rider must be prepared just in case his view is blocked on the approach. Take note of the stringing of the course and imagine a crowd of people possibly blocking your view. Always choose a high landmark in this situation – a low one would disappear in the crowd. The horse may also be rather fazed by a crowd of people and lose concentration – all this must be taken into account when assessing a fence's difficulty. Riders have to be able to react quickly to avert a problem if they feel the horse freeze on seeing a mass of people.

35. Two horses jumping the same fence on totally different angles. The bay horse is jumping the fence well, whereas the grey is slightly diving over it (note the insecure lower leg of both riders with the weight not truly in the stirrup). It is always advisable, particularly with a novice horse, to jump a trakehner at right-angles to the ditch (as the bay horse is doing). A fence with a ditch below presents a problem in itself and any difficult fence should be jumped straight and not on the angle.

36. With a mass of trees to pass through, any misjudgement of line would be disastrous. The horse has to be able to see a way through, and the rider must have carefully chosen his line when walking the course and stuck to it when approaching on his horse. Note the upright body on the approach to ensure that the horse stays in front of the rider. The rider has not collapsed on her horse's neck over the fence, so she is in a position to keep the horse going forward through subsequent elements.

Shadows cast may throw a false ground-line – these all need inspecting and considering.

After the first walk round, you will have a general picture in your mind of the pattern of the course. You have to decide how this pattern will suit your horse. It will influence which way you choose to jump some of the option fences. A 'friendly' course is one where, if there is a difficult fence, it is followed by a let-up fence so that the horse's confidence is always kept buoyant. A more difficult track is one where difficult, demanding fences follow each other. This is what makes Badminton the most difficult three-day event. There are few, if any, let-up fences. The problem for the horse then is that if he makes a mistake, or has a fright at a fence, there is no easy fence to restore his faith and confidence. Eventually, after being asked question after question, he will finally say, 'I've had enough.' Horses vary in character and it is vital that you understand your horse. You must know how he will react to one big fence followed by another. It may be that you will have to opt for an easier option, if possible, at one of these so that your horse does not lose confidence. A very bold horse probably will not worry and prefers to have a challenge, but a more timid creature may need some understanding treatment to keep up his spirits.

The ground conditions and terrain affect how punishing some fences, such as drops, can be for the horse. If a horse is punished by a drop onto hard ground, or by jumping into the face of a bank,

37. This going is deep and sticky, which can have a serious effect on the horse as he lands. As you know yourself, if you get your feet stuck you fall forwards – the effect on the horse is the same. If his front feet get stuck in deep going as he lands, all the weight carries on forward and he can peck, stumble or even fall. If the rider's weight is forward too, the effect can be disastrous and the rider can actually *make* the horse fall on landing. This is a situation most often found on a cross-country course, but sometimes the show-jumping gets deep and sticky too. If the rider sits back too soon then, the horse may be forced to drop his hindquarters early and have his fences down behind. The rider must allow the horse to follow through the bascule before drawing his shoulders back to help the balance.

Imagine, too, the effect of jumping out of this sort of going. The power required is much greater. Greater emphasis is placed on balance, impulsion and rhythm. The odd mistake can be overcome when the conditions are perfect, but when they are dire, a far greater stress is put on correct training and horsemanship. Take note of how many more faults are shown on the scoreboard when it is pouring with rain and the going is treacherous than when it is a sunny day with good going.

For a young, inexperienced horse it may be that he is not ready to cope with jumping out of such going. Obviously it depends on the size and difficulty of the course and he has to learn some day how to cope with adverse conditions. The rider must find a balance between allowing his horse to learn and 'grow up' and frightening him through slipping or finding the going too deep to jump well. Hunting is one of the best ways to introduce a horse to bad going. In his enthusiasm to follow everyone else, the horse ceases to worry about the ground, and after stumbling, tripping and heaving himself through deep going starts to discover the easiest way to cope with it. In his excitement he is unlikely to remember a slightly awkward jump, but any loss of confidence can be restored by schooling at home.

It is much more difficult to rekindle enthusiasm and confidence if it is lost at a competition. If the going is bad, it may be better to wait for another day. There is also the injury factor to consider. Injuries happen even when the going is good, and are more likely to occur when the opposite is the case. Although we should not wrap our horses up in cotton wool, if we want them to last it is worth looking after them. If you do decide that the going is fit to run on, alter the pace accordingly. Again, you cannot crawl round, but if the speed is reduced – like driving in bad weather – you are more likely to get to the end of your journey in one piece.

A good event horse must be able to cope with a variety of going and this is all part of his training. You do not work all year towards a three-day event only to be thrown into a frenzy because the going is not perfect. In the production of an event horse, a balance must be found between caring for and cosseting him. Your attitude must be all the more positive if the going is not good. If you ride timidly, then the horse will respond accordingly. The more strongly you ride, without over-riding and so losing the balance, the more you will keep the horse together with his hocks under him. Extra balance and impulsion will give the horse the ability to cope with any going. All you have to remember is to keep hold of your horse (without restricting), keeping him between hand and leg and making sure that you are ready to switch to the safety seat – heels down, lower leg forward ready to brace any impact and head up – to counteract any loss of balance. This comes from practice and experience. If you never go cross-country when the weather is bad, you will never learn this vital part of horsemanship. There are many fair-weather riders – absolutely fine, I don't blame them! – but if you want to be a successful competitor, then you have to take the rough with the smooth and get wet and muddy!

he will eventually associate cross-country fences with discomfort. If, as he gets older, he finds these sorts of fences increasingly uncomfortable to jump, he will slowly lose his enthusiasm for the job and start to stop. Try to avoid undue wear and tear. Of course the horse has to jump a certain number of drop fences and fences which are not altogether 'fun' for him – this is all part of the game – but by minimising the punishing fences, you are prolonging the horse's eventing lifetime.

Ground conditions can dramatically change the nature of a fence and must be taken into consideration. It may be that the ground either side of a fence will deteriorate during the day and ground that was fine when you walked the course becomes heavy or sticky by the time you ride it. You should inspect any suspect ground and, if in doubt, avoid jumping anywhere which risks injury or a problem due to the ground. It may be that by choosing fresh ground, you can avoid the worst, but this line must be carefully walked. By jumping anywhere other than the middle of a fence, you are increasing the chance of a run-out. Precision riding is required when jumping off-centre or on the angle. There is no room for error.

When deciding which route to take, you must weigh up the various factors in your mind. You must judge the risk factor – is the risk of 20 penalties worth it? Are a couple of time faults preferable? Is the punishing drop worth the seconds saved? Is it worth testing the horse's courage by jumping the straight way over consecutive demanding fences, or should his morale be boosted by an easier jump? Will the confined space created by the crowd give enough room to jump the fence safely? Is the so-called quick route *really* quicker? Would it not take as little time to nip round the corner and jump the longer route? Will the dappling light shining through the trees affect the horse's judgement of the fence? There are a multitude of questions you should ask yourself. It is vital that you have answered them all positively before you set off on the horse. Any dithering will cause problems. By all means, have an open mind, but know which option you are taking well before you start on the approach to each fence. If you waver on the approach, the horse will be given a vague message which invites a problem.

This mental approach is all part of the walking of a course. It is not just as simple as walking round to see where the track takes you, jumping the fences as you come to them. There is so much involved in the walking of any course. Every course is different;

every horse is different, and the skill of the rider is in deciding which is the best, safest and quickest route for him.

If time allows, it is useful to be able to watch some horses jumping some of the more difficult fences. In some ways, this may be alarming because if you see a series of moderately ridden horses, badly prepared to jump the fences, your heart will sink. It may appear that the fence is impossible to jump neatly and safely. It is important for your morale that you see a horse jump through a combination or over a tricky fence without any trouble, and indeed with ease, otherwise you may ride the fence without confidence. Then you too will have problems if you do not ride positively. You can only learn whether the way you have decided to jump a fence is suitable for your horse if you see a horse of similar type jumping it. If you have a long-striding horse and watch short-striding horses struggle to jump something, you will learn little (as with the show-jumping course). Assess carefully what you see, and rather than get depressed and gloomy when horses make mistakes, work out what went wrong. Was it rider error? Is the fence too difficult and punishing to jump for your own or your horse's experience? Try to see an experienced rider over the fence before making a final judgement.

Before riding any course, try to find half-an-hour to sit quietly to go over the course in your mind. This is called visualisation. It is not just a case of running through the fences, but of riding every inch of the way. Imagine the approaches to every fence, how you will ride them, what pace you will want to establish and when (you may need to resort to looking at your programme, where you should have written down landmarks for altering pace, etc.). Visualise jumping every fence; remember the landings, the drops, turns or any undulating ground. Picture the long gallops, the rough patches of going if there are any, the turns into various fences or any turns generally. Go through the course in your mind and negotiate all the fences in a positive way. Eliminate any problems by imagining what you would do to prevent them. You should finish the whole exercise in your mind by riding through the finish and completing. You should then be mentally prepared to ride the course with positive attack.

This time for yourself is necessary so that you can compose yourself and concentrate totally on the task ahead. You can then go out and ride the course without hesitation. You will be feeling confident about which lines you are taking and what will decide you should you have to make a change of plan. It is so important not to set off to the start of the cross-country in a flustered state. You need all the concentration possible when riding a course and correct mental preparation is important. The bigger and more complicated the track, the more important this is.

This visualisation is an important part of riding, not just of jumping a cross-country course. You should experiment with it before riding a dressage test or a show-jumping round too. It is enormously useful in channelling your thoughts and making you *think* about what you are doing. With jumping in particular, where a lapse in concentration may mean the loss of many marks (as opposed to one or two in a dressage test), you cannot jump a good round unless you have put some thought into it. There is always so much to think about that the more that is crystallised in your mind, the easier the task will be.

The thought and consideration behind jumping a fence is all part of its successful negotiation and the actual physical act of riding it.

Warming-up

Warming-up for the cross-country is as important as for any other discipline. The horse must be prepared both physically and mentally for the task ahead. He will have had a certain amount of work already for the dressage and show-jumping at a one-day event, so he will not need more than 15 or 20 minutes' preparation. If you are doing just cross-country, then the horse will need longer preliminary work of trotting and suppling before you start cantering.

After walking quietly down to the start, having checked your girths, you should then have a brisk canter on both reins. You should vary the pace, ensuring that the horse responds to both upward and downward aids and turns easily either way. You need not worry about outline, but merely balance. As with any jumping, the horse must be able to have freedom of his head and neck, so do not fall into the trap of restricting him during the warm-up.

After you have worked in canter, you should increase pace again to give a few strides of gallop – make sure you are not disrupting other competitors. You are not looking for a full gallop, but merely an increase of pace to gallop then back to canter. Your horse should be obedient in all paces and not become ill-mannered and resistant in an increased pace. Your horse does not want tiring out, but made attentive and responsive at a faster pace.

You should then proceed to the practice fence and jump it from a canter a couple of times before moving up a gear and jumping it at an increased speed. This does not mean that the horse jumps the fence long and flat, but that he becomes sharper and quicker on his feet. Take note of the flagging of the practice fence and make sure you do not jump it the wrong way. If there are two practice fences, jump them both. If possible, jump the fences on the angle to prepare for any angled rails on the course itself. Jump both ways on the angle, i.e. right to left and left to right. Provided that the horse jumps without hesitation off both reins, you should only need to angle the fences once. Do be careful that other competitors realise that you are approaching the fence to jump it – approaching from the side may be misleading and may cause a collision.

Probably half-a-dozen practice jumps will be enough – two slowly, two at a quicker pace and two on the angle. You need the horse to be alert and attentive but without being sweaty and blowing. Obviously this depends on the horse and his experience – a spooky horse may need more jumping than a bold one. To keep both you and your horse 'on the boil', try to time your warming-up to be near your time to go. Walking round for ages can be nerve-wracking! If there is a delay, and you have to wait for a long time, make sure you have a rug thrown over the horse's quarters and keep him gently on the move. A quick pop over the practice fence just before you are called to the start box puts horse and rider on their toes and in the right frame of mind to attack the course.

Picture the course in your mind as you wander round during your warm-up and try not to think negatively about any fence. Imagine how you will ride the more difficult ones and imagine yourself sailing over without problems. You can soon convince yourself that you will not get further than the fourth fence if you allow your mind to look on the gloomy side. *Make* yourself look confidently towards jumping every fence well and it is surprising how that attitude will transfer itself to the way you ride and to the horse itself. Your mood will be transmitted immediately to the horse, so take a grip of yourself and think positive!

Chapter 5

Roads and Tracks and Steeplechase

Roads and tracks

Although no jumping is involved on Phases A and C – the roads and tracks of a three-day event – they do exert a great influence on the cross-country and even on the show-jumping. Their role is to test the horse's fitness and stamina. Phase A is the warm-up period for Phase B, the steeplechase, and it is shorter than Phase C, which is the recovery period. The total length of A and C varies according to the standard of the event, ranging from nearly 8,000 metres for Novice to nearly 14,000 metres for Advanced.

If a horse finishes exhausted at the end of the speed and endurance day, apart from the fact that it is an appalling sight, it will in the short term reduce his chances of jumping a clear round in the show-jumping the following day, and in the long term affect him psychologically for the future. The rider must plan carefully how to ride Phases A, B and C as well as D. It is advisable to view the roads and tracks twice. After the briefing, it is normal for a fleet of vehicles to drive round the roads and track and any announcements regarding them are then made. It is important to concentrate and to disregard distractions and the chattering which invariably goes on in the vehicles. Note the terrain, the going, the kilometre markers and the compulsory turning flags. Mark them on your map so that you can check them later. It is quite normal for at least one competitor to be eliminated, especially at Novice level, for missing a flag.

Having driven round, you will have an idea of pace – i.e. where you can canter, where you have to walk or where you have to give the horse a breather on an uphill stretch. You should decide what studs you can use – ideally the same ones should be used throughout all four phases to avoid changing them in the ten-minute box. If road work is unavoidable, road studs are the answer because they give some grip for the chase as well as keeping the holes clean.

You may ride Phases A and C prior to the actual day of competition. You can get far more idea of 'feel' on a horse than in a vehicle and you will be able to test the going and decide how demanding the gradients are. Many people look for short-cuts on the roads and tracks. It is rare that there are any to be found – the organisers are aware of this! Should you find one, ask yourself the following questions before embarking on saving a few seconds. Am I missing any flags? Is the going good with no hidden hazards in long grass, for example? Would I do any damage to lawns, crops, etc.? Is it really worth it? Words of caution! During all the fitness work with his horse, the rider has ample time to practise using a stop-watch. It is so important that you know exactly how to work your watches and how to work out your timings. Once the competition starts, there is so much to think about that it is crucial that operating the stop-watch buttons is second nature to you. If you are panicking about how to use your watch, it will distract you from more important matters and you will lose concentration and make silly mistakes. It is important to keep looking and checking your watches on the roads and tracks. Watches do sometimes break down (ensure that your batteries are new), so always have a back-up watch and keep your eye on them both.

Your horse will probably be keen and exuberant on Phase A. Keep him as settled as possible, trying to relax him so that he does

38. An eager, well-balanced horse trotting on the roads and tracks. The rider has the horse on a contact but not forced into a shape. The horse is being given every chance to take the minimum out of himself.

not expend nervous energy. Give him a quick whizz at a previously chosen place where the going is good. This clears his 'tubes' and gets him on the ball for the steeplechase. Avoid fighting your horse on this phase – try to switch him off as best you can.

39. Sloppy riding can make the roads and tracks much harder work for the horse. In order to use up minimum energy, the horse must be kept balanced – if he has to balance himself without the help of the rider this is harder work for him. Similarly, the horse should not be worked as such by being forced into a shape. He should be allowed to carry himself in the way he finds the most comfortable and the rider should make his load as easy as possible. Standing up in your stirrups eases the weight on the horse's back but you must be used to this otherwise you will find that your legs will be killing you and will be totally ineffective when it comes to the cross-country! I would recommend practising standing up in the stirrups at home on exercise as an excellent way of strengthening the legs. The rider must be as fit as his horse.

Work out your times so that you arrive with a minute in hand before the steeplechase to have your girths checked and find out how the course is riding. After the steeplechase, you should allow time for the horse to recover his breathing during the first kilometre on Phase C. This phase in particular needs thoughtful riding. The horse must be given every chance to recover. Pick easy ground for him and help him by balancing him: do not make him 'work' by putting him in an outline. Let him carry himself as he is most comfortable. Keep the weight off his back – some people even dismount, but I find that standing up in your stirrups as much as you can is sufficient. (You have to be fit to be able to do this!) Preserving energy in a horse is like driving a car when it is running out of petrol – you must avoid either accelerating or braking hard. With a horse, keep the rhythm and make no sudden changes of pace or direction. Avoid deep going or ground that is changeable – this breaks the rhythm and is tiring for the horse.

Do not forget to trot the final yards at the end of Phase C towards the inspection panel so that they can check that your horse is sound. It is tiresome to have to be asked to do it again. As the panel check your horse's heart and breathing, ask whether they need to see him again before you set off on Phase D.

Do not underestimate the influence of Phases A and C. If the horse uses excess energy in these phases, he will be drained of energy when it is needed and if the rider worries unduly about his timings or stop-watch, his concentration will be directed away from more important issues. Remember that clear rounds are part of a big picture.

Steeplechase

Sandwiched between the two phases of roads and tracks is the important steeplechase, Phase B. It is part of the speed and endurance test of a three-day event and plays an influential role. The pace is fast and for many horses it may even be flat out. The faster the horse gallops, the more important it is to balance him and to maintain a rhythm. It is a phase which is sadly neglected and, particularly at the lower-level events, there are many poor spectacles to be seen.

The essence of a good, safe steeplechase phase is rhythm and balance – the same as for any jumping. The difference is the pace. The speed means that the horse has the impetus to stand off further which, given the nature of steeplechase fences, it is safe to do. Constructed of brush, and sloping, the fences are quite forgiving. It is unnecessary to alter the pace and 'set up' the horse in the same way as one would do for a more solid obstacle. In the steeplechase, the horse must keep the same pace and jump out of his stride. Provided that he is balanced, he should find this easy. The rider's task is to ensure that he himself is balanced and that he does not interefere adversely with his horse's balance. It is imperative that the horse does not change this balance during the last few strides to take-off. If any re-balancing is necessary, the rider must do this at least half-a-dozen strides away from the fence. If the horse's balance is altered by the rider interfering during the last take-off strides, he has no chance of altering his stride pattern to meet the fence correctly. Provided that the horse is balanced and in rhythm, he can adjust himself for take-off. If the rider sends him into the fence on a long, flat stride, thereby putting him on his forehand, the horse will be unable to alter his stride if the rider has made a mistake.

We are privileged in this country to have some of the best jump jockeys in the world and they should be studied carefully. John Francome and Peter Scudamore (both now retired), Richard Dunwoody and many of their contemporaries are true horsemen – which was more than proved a few years ago when some of them rode round the Gatcombe horse trials Advanced course on borrowed horses. Putting balance and rhythm into practice, they made it look so easy and as if they had ridden round the course many times before – it quite showed up many event riders!

Riding at speed puts an emphasis on balance and any alteration of balance is generally paid for by a fall. Study Dunwoody, for example, and see how still he keeps, how he is always in balance himself, allowing his horse maximum use of his head and neck to preserve balance in anxious moments. In fact, if you look at photographs of any of the top jockeys, you will note how balanced they are and how, despite jumping at speed, they maintain their own equilibrium. They keep their heads up (you never see a good jockey looking down over a fence) and the weight is firmly in the stirrup. Once a jockey is unbalanced, he will fall off if the horse makes the slightest mistake.

The faster a horse goes, the further forward his centre of balance will be. This is why it is necessary to shorten the stirrups for the steeplechase. Many riders ride with too long a stirrup to be able to stay in balance. The length of stirrup for the 'chase should be shorter than for cross-country. As with everything, this should be practised at home. Try using a racing saddle sometimes; I make all my pupils ride in racing saddles on occasions, doing flat work and jumping too. It helps the balance enormously and makes them more aware of loss of balance because they cannot grip with their knees. They have to find true balance. This is what so many riders lack. Balance can be improved with practice. True balance is dependent upon a good position so this emphasises how important it is to sit correctly and work hard to establish a correct position and seat.

I would advise riders to hold their reins in a bridge. This gives the hands more security and the rider can rest on the bridge while galloping on the flat. It is much easier to slip the reins and shorten them again if a bridge is held. It is easier to keep a horse straight and turning is more controlled with the help of bridged reins. It may seem strange initially, but I, for one, would feel totally lost without a bridge when working a horse at speed. Another aspect of riding to practise at home – try schooling a horse with bridged reins – it will make you aware of how straight the horse must be.

An unattractive sight at three-day events is a rider bobbling about on his or her horse's back, with long stirrups and flapping reins. The horse is being given no help at all in directing him or keeping any sort of balance or rhythm. The horse should gallop straight on a steady contact, with the rider sitting very still (all riders, however tall, should appear neat in their position). The rider's weight should remain as stable as possible and there should be minimum body movement, particularly over a fence. Being in forward position anyway, the rider barely needs to move, but just allows the horse's jump to fold him at the hips. Again, study the jockeys – they hardly move position at all. This is all the more evident over hurdles, when they maintain position unless the horse makes a mistake. Over fences, the body weight is braced against the stirrup to absorb any shock, such as the horse pecking or hitting a fence. But even then there is little movement of the body. This is something we event riders should try to emulate.

Few people make the effort to go schooling (ask for some help from a successful rider who has ridden over fences in races – most people are delighted to help) over steeplechase fences. It is part of the training of the event horse (and rider). A trainer of steeple-chasers schools his horses over fences and we should school ours too. The steeplechase phase is important. To perform it well, using minimum energy, requires practice and training. You have

40. A good position on the steeplechase (*above*) with the rider in a balanced forward position. Note the weight in the heel, the head up and the straight line from the horse's mouth through the rein to the hand. Compare this with the rider below (this time on the cross-country). The lower leg is a fraction far back and the upper body too far forward – the rider's head is almost in the horse's mane. This position will require more body movement in the re-balancing process.

to learn your own horse's cruising speed and how he copes with jumping at speed. It is probably not necessary to school more than once per season, and maybe not at all with an experienced campaigner, but for an inexperienced combination it is crucial.

Steeplechase schooling is exhilarating provided it is done correctly. Make sure you only school on good ground and over well-built fences. Most racehorse trainers hire out their schooling fences. The horse must be wearing good quality tack and all the necessary kit such as boots, breastplate, safe girths and reins either stitched or with a buckle and a martingale if used. The rider must wear a crash cap, body protector and correct footwear. The horse will need a minimum of twenty minutes' warm-up walking and trotting. He should then have a canter for a couple or so furlongs at a brisk pace. Then, having checked your girths, you are ready to start. It is more beneficial to go up, say, three or four fences twice than to do, say, eight all in one go. You can assess what, if anything, went wrong the first time and you have an opportunity to correct it on the second run. There is less risk of your horse injuring himself if he is not allowed to get tired. Going up the fences twice is the same principle as interval training – the horse has time to recover in between. Concentrate on getting into the rhythm as quickly as possible and maintaining the same rhythm throughout. Concentrate on your position – keeping your eyes and head up, your weight in your heels and staying absolutely in balance, waiting for the horse to take off before closing the hip angle to form the forward swing. Brace against the stirrup as you land and pick up the rhythm immediately after each fence. Keep the horse up to the bridle and do not let him drop behind the contact. Hold a bridge and keep your hands low and still, following the movement as necessary.

41. An immaculate steeplechase position – heels down, seat low, head up and the horse being given the necessary freedom without losing the contact. A picture of perfect balance and harmony.

Whenever you pull up, whether it is in competition or at home, always do so straight and without losing the contact. This keeps the horse balanced and is less likely to cause damage to tendons. This is all the more important when a horse is tired. If he is pulled up in a circle, it can place excess strain on one point and give the horse 'a leg'. Keeping the horse straight keeps the weight distribution more even.

---

42. Injuries occur more often when a horse is tired. More horses break down at the end of a race than at the beginning. An event rider may be riding a tired horse at the end of a cross-country round (fitness is, of course, important to avoid this as much as possible) – perhaps 'leg-weary' would be a better expression to use. Certainly, at the end of a three-day event track the horse will be tired, but he should not be tired at the end of a one-day event. The finish is part of the competition – failing to pass between the flags means elimination. Obviously, when against the clock one wants to make up as much time as possible and, without a fence to worry about, the temptation is to put the foot flat down. Alas, in doing so, many riders forget all about balance. An all-too-common sight is a horse being kicked flat out from the last fence, the rider with reins flapping and legs at work and the horse flying headlong on his forehand to the finish.

A horse should be kept between hand and leg and kept balanced. Some of the best jockeys are able to keep their horse balanced without needing to resort to the reins but this is an art. When riding for the finishing line, do not drop everything and flop around on the horse's back. Keep your position and encourage the horse to lengthen his stride without hurling him onto his forehand and losing balance.

I would recommend that anyone who wishes to compete at a serious level eventing should ride out for a local racehorse trainer. By riding short and riding horses at speed, your own balance and the feeling of keeping your horse balanced will improve enormously. It is only once you increase pace that the true meaning of balance sinks in and it is the ability to keep a horse balanced by the influence of your own balance and position which is so important. With short stirrups, you cannot rely on your knees or legs but must use your balance to good effect. You will be amazed how this will help to improve your ability to keep your event horse balanced as well as increasing your knowledge of pace and speed.

Do not forget the importance of pulling up correctly – gradually and straight rather than abruptly or by whizzing the horse round, which invites injury as well as putting unnecessary strain on a horse when he deserves more sympathetic treatment. Watch how jockeys pull up after a race. They take a long time – especially the Flat jockeys whose horses have been going very fast. This winding down is important if you are to avoid damage. If a horse is asked to slow down too quickly, he will put undue strain on his forelegs and shoulders. Immediate damage may not be obvious but the effect will be cumulative. Keep your weight off the horse's back as you pull up and do not flop down onto him just because you are tired or disappointed. When you do resume your seat in the saddle, sit lightly – your horse deserves that.

When riding the steeplechase phase in competition, the aim is to complete the course without time faults yet expending minimum energy. It is important to ride the shortest route. Take careful note of the turns when you walk the course. It may be necessary to swing slightly wide at one point of a corner so that you can cut close on the second part. By hugging the rails all the way you may make the bends too tight and the horse will have to swing out wide as he loses balance. Take note of any undulation – balance is lost easily when travelling at speed. The quicker you get into the stride, the quicker you pick up rhythm after each fence. So many people lose time by taking ages to pick up their pace. They dawdle after each fence, swing wide round each corner or show-jump the fences. You must keep coming to the fences and jump them out of the horse's stride – there is no time to fiddle around looking for strides. Slowing down and speeding up also takes more out of the horse, so try to keep an even rhythm and pace.

You will have decided upon a halfway point. Check your watch, but keep up the gallop. It is easy to think you have time in hand, but although you do not want to be faster than required – there is no advantage at all; in fact it is detrimental – you do not want to pick up unnecessary time faults. You can always slow down a little after the last. There are some instances when a few time faults are advisable, for example when the weather conditions are poor, the going is not good or your horse would be

43. Cornering on the steeplechase. The horse is hugging the rails and wasting no ground or time. The rider is looking ahead and is riding with a purpose. The position is good, although from this angle it looks as though the rider would find it easier and more comfortable with a shorter stirrup, which allows a more secure position.

struggling to make the time and to do so would be to run him off his feet. Remember that there is a long way to go after the 'chase. A few time penalties are preferable to an exhausted or lame horse. Apart from the cross-country, there is also the show-jumping to come the following day. You must reserve enough energy for that vital phase. A show-jumping fault of five penalties is costly. One time fault on the 'chase is probably considerably less so.

Riding a steeplechase on your own is far more difficult than riding in a point-to-point. When racing, the other horses draw you into the fences and give you more impetus. When on your own, the horse is unlikely to pull much so you are not drawn to the fences in the same way. It is worthwhile schooling with another horse to give your horse more incentive and enthusiasm. It is normally easier to school upsides than on your own for the same reason. A horse which takes you to a fence (but in control!) is much easier to ride than one off the bridle.

If the horse is not 'up to your hand' and 'taking you' to the fences, he is not going forward. Remember: forward + balance = rhythm. Rhythm gives the power to lengthen and shorten the stride. So the moment the horse stops 'taking you', you know that you will be under-powered at take-off. If the take-off point is then not correct, the horse will be unable to alter. This is one of the reasons why tired horses fall more often than fresh ones – they drop the bridle. You will see National Hunt jockeys really get hold of tired horses to try to keep them up to the bridle. You will never see a loose rein, unless perhaps in the final finishing strides of a frantically close-run race.

The old adage of '*keep hold and keep kicking*' is not too far wrong. By doing so you will keep both balance and rhythm, but if you do one and not the other you will lose both. If you feel the horse coming off the bridle, kick him up to your hand about eight strides away from the fence, but do maintain rhythm and balance.

Steeplechase and show-jumping seem to be everyone's weak links, but this is purely because of lack of practice. Do take any opportunity to ride out for a racehorse trainer – it will be enormously beneficial.

Chapter 6

Pace

'He's a wonderful judge of pace' – what does it mean?

Deciding which pace you should adopt is rather like learning what speed to drive a car with no speedometer. It is something that comes with experience in both instances. A driver who has recently passed his driving test will be far less able to judge his speed than an experienced driver. A 'professional' driver will be more capable of judging speed than a weekend driver. A rider will be exactly the same. A novice rider will find it difficult to judge pace. He will learn to feel pace on one horse after some time, but the moment he rides a different horse he will take time to adjust. An experienced rider will quickly assess the pace of a new horse, just like a professional driver who can switch from car to car and adjust accordingly. Someone who has ridden for years, who merely hacks and takes life gently in a non-competitive way, is comparable to the weekend driver. Both would find judging pace difficult.

Practice. This is a word which creeps in on a regular basis, but this is the only way to learn. In jumping, the show-jumping pace is more easily learnt because it can be worked on every day in the school. The working canter is the show-jumping canter. The cross-country speed is more difficult to gauge. Not only is it impractical to gallop the horse too much, but also the cross-country pace varies so much. It depends upon individual fences, the terrain, the going, the weather conditions, the difficulty of the course and the experience of horse and rider. Some riders, such as Mark Todd, can take a young horse quickly but safely. A more novice rider would have to take the same horse much slower. It all boils down to the ability to balance the horse and present him correctly and in rhythm at his fences.

Initially when riding cross-country, work on a pace which you and your horse find comfortable. In between fences, you can slide the horse on faster, but try to keep the transitions smooth from canter to gallop and back again. Avoid heaving and hauling, booting and shoving. Aim for minimum movement and smoothness, maintaining rhythm and balance. Cross-country speed at Novice level is fast. You should not be aiming to get within the time with a young horse or as an inexperienced rider. Far better to pick up time faults but have a smooth, rhythmical round. This is far more likely to prepare you and your horse for the future than battling flat out over 3′ 6″. The horse does not learn to look at what he is doing and will become strong and therefore difficult to balance. In the early stages of any career, whether it be the horse's or the rider's, be patient.

Steeplechase pace is the fastest required from an event horse. Once the rider has learnt the speed required, it is not difficult to master because there is no alteration of pace. The horse must keep up the same gallop and does not have to slow down for turns or be set up for solid fences. Like show-jumping, the pace is more or less constant. It is the cross-country phase which requires most understanding of pace.

The best way to check the speed required for steeplechase is to measure a kilometre in a large, flat field (with good going) and then time yourself over that distance. You will then get the feeling of the pace necessary, bearing in mind that you might lose some time over the fences unless you meet them on a good stride. You must remember to pick up the speed quickly on landing, particularly if you meet a fence on a shortened stride. You can lose seconds per fence in this way, as you will if the horse dwells in the air. If you give the horse a kick as he lands, he will soon learn to be quick away from his fences – the same applies to cross-country obstacles.

The object of a cross-country course builder is to provide a challenge for horse and rider. Depending on the level of competition, this challenge varies in difficulty. The course builder designs a course which is a mixture of technical and straightforward, galloping fences and the rider has to pit his wits against the course to complete it without either jumping or time penalties. This is the aim for the experienced rider on a horse well enough schooled to respond.

Pace, of course, has most influence on the time of a cross-country round. However, riding flat out round a course is not good riding. A good time is better achieved by a rider maintaining an even rhythm throughout and riding an economical route. If you study our top event riders such as Mark Todd or Ginny Elliot, they never appear to be in a hurry. They keep up a relentless pace, which is not flat out, and also an unchanging rhythm. This has two advantages as a way of riding. Firstly, it means that balance is rarely lost, and secondly, the horse takes far less out of himself – vitally important at a three-day event. The faster you go, the more you have to slow up for turns and tricky fences. It is almost impossible to keep a round fluid and smooth if the horse has to change pace from very fast to slow. Trying to balance the horse throughout dramatic changes of pace is also very difficult.

To jump a solid fence safely at speed requires an experienced rider on a well-trained horse. For the average horse and rider it is, for the spectator at least, a heart-in-mouth moment. It is a hit-and-miss affair which, when the day comes when it is a 'miss' (and that day certainly will come) will result in a fall. There is only a certain length of time that luck will last. The whole purpose of training and schooling and practising is so that luck is not the prime ingredient for success. We all need an absence of bad luck — but winning should not be entirely due to good luck. It is the result of hours of hard work and training of both the rider and the horse.

Horses only have a limited mileage in them, so in order to preserve them we have to be careful that with our competitive spirits we do not abuse them. It is a sad sight to see horses galloping flat out round cross country courses week after week or when the going is poor. Particularly with a young horse, it is imperative that he is not rushed or hurried, but that the pace is gradually increased so that he hardly notices he is travelling more quickly. On occasions, it may be necessary to 'put your foot down', but there is no reason why the horse should not have a quiet run next time out. There is always another day, another occasion — this seems to be forgotten by riders who hurtle their horses round rock-hard ground or hock-deep mud. It is pure ignorance of the potential injuries that can be caused by such ground — injuries which would cause permanent damage or mean that the horse has to spend a year or more resting. Furthermore, bad ground can wreck a horse's confidence and morale. Jumping drop fences onto hard ground gives any horse an uncomfortable feeling which is unlikely to be forgotten. These bad experiences may eventually cause a horse to question his courage. Many horses refuse at drop fences — young horses jump from blissful ignorance at the outset of their careers, but may eventually learn to associate drop fences with discomfort unless nurtured to a degree. Never forget, it is speed that kills. By slowing down, you reduce the jarring and keep the horse happy. I am not suggesting that you should pamper your horse and cosset him. I am saying that you should take into account the number of times you compete your horse, the going, the horse's experience, the difficulty of the course or terrain and the horse's fitness.

While you walk the course, you should be thinking about how you will ride it. You should decide not only where you will choose your lines for each fence, but also how to avoid any bad going. Every outing should teach you and your horse something so that you are building up confidence and experience to compete at a higher level should you want to. By riding small courses correctly, you are setting the correct base for successfully negotiating higher levels.

Stop-watches are much in evidence today. Although at a three-day event they are essential for roads and tracks, they should only be necessary as a check for the pace of steeplechase and cross-country. It is a mistake to rely on your stop-watch. You should try to learn to feel your pace and judge it without needing to resort endlessly to a watch.

The rider's position is all-important. A well-balanced rider (one with a good position) will be far easier for the horse to carry than someone who is relying on his horse for balance. Try giving somebody a piggy back who drags on your neck or wriggles around. They seem much heavier and harder work to carry than someone who keeps still and holds their own balance without having to hang onto you. For the horse, the feeling is the same. A well-balanced rider will ride light, whereas someone with a poor position will ride heavily because he relies on the horse's back to support his weight. If the weight is truly in the stirrup, then it is not on the horse's back. The horse will have free use of his head and neck provided that the rider is not relying on the reins to support him. This is all the more important in anxious moments – the most difficult time for the rider to maintain balance. Anyone can perch on a horse provided that everything goes to plan. The good rider is the one who preserves his balance when things go wrong. This only comes from, firstly, a good seat and, secondly, practice and experience. Many times a horse is almost forced to fall due to his rider's weight being wrongly placed. This is a common fault with a less experienced rider – by flopping forward onto the horse's neck, he unbalances the horse and down he goes.

The ability to maintain an even pace relates to the fitness of horse and rider. Keeping up a relentless rhythm, whatever the pace, demands fitness from both. The fitter the combination, the safer they will be – many falls or losses of balance and the inability to recover from mistakes hinge to a great degree on the level of fitness. An unfit horse or rider will lose strength and speed of reaction. This can prove disastrous.

You can practise keeping an even pace at home for show-jumping by working over related distances. If you build a line of fences three or four strides apart at a distance of 19 or 23 yards and then canter round and pick out parts of the line to jump on the oblique, keeping an even pace and rhythm, you will soon get the feel of the necessary pace for show-jumping (see Diagram 10, page 42). When jumping at home, try to string a number of fences together rather than just jumping single obstacles. It is, after all, a course of fences at canter which is the objective, so practise picking up the rhythm and balance as soon as possible on landing, and then jumping another fence from that canter. Avoid jumping a fence, then allowing the horse to stumble into a trot with lavish patting and praise. Discipline your horse and yourself only to change pace when you decide rather than automatically flopping into walk. A fence should be thought of as an incidental to the canter pace which neither interrupts nor changes the rhythm and balance. There should be no change of pace unless instructed.

Even if you do not jump more than one fence at a time, ensure that you canter a circle after (more important than before) a fence to practise picking up balance and rhythm. A fence will disrupt the balance – hence the need to circle afterwards rather than before. When you land, give the horse time to find his own balance by being in a perfect position yourself. On no account should the horse land and 'wait for the grab' when the rider tries to balance the horse with his hand. This only causes stiffness and tension and the horse may try to run from the restriction. When you land over a fence, make sure you go with the horse, even if you think he is going too fast. Balance will only be restored by the horse bringing his hocks underneath him.

Once a rider can master jumping simple, small fences correctly, he should then be able to progress without problems to jumping bigger or more difficult fences or from a faster pace because he understands the principles of rhythm and balance. Without this basic knowledge, safe, successful jumping at speed will be impossible.

Chapter 7

The Cross-Country

For this chapter I have chosen a variety of photographs to illustrate the right and potentially hazardous ways of riding different types of cross-country fence.

For any cross-country riding, I would recommend that you should always carry a whip and wear spurs. Cross-country presents a variety of 'surprises' and even the most honest horse may need the occasional encouragement and reminder that he must jump a particularly suspicious-looking fence. A quick flip of the whip at an opportune moment (behind the saddle with the hand off the rein) can often make the difference between a clear round and twenty penalties. The object of the rider is to complete a cross-country course as smoothly and rhythmically as possible, so taking the minimum out of his horse. It is vital to learn how to do this if a three-day event is the final objective.

Having walked the course, the rider knows precisely (or should do!) which lines he will take and the pace at which he will approach each fence. All he has to do then is to put it into practice. The more difficult and technical the fence, or the shorter the distance in a combination, the more setting-up and re-balancing is required. The main problems stem from riders leaving their preparations for a fence too late. A coffin, for example, needs preparing for in plenty of time to ensure that the horse is in a slow, bouncy, balanced pace yet full of impulsion. It is impossible for a novice horse to change from a fast canter/gallop to the necessary approach for a coffin in a few strides. The better trained the horse, the quicker this transition can be, therefore the more experienced and better-schooled horses will be quicker cross-country. A horse must never be pushed more quickly than his capabilities at the time allow.

Every fence needs some preparation in the alteration of the balance and the transferral of weight from the forehand to the hindquarters. You can think of it as a change of gear. A car cruises in fifth gear; a straightforward fence will mean a change down to fourth, a more upright type of fence might require third gear, a coffin second gear, a step down into water first gear. The engine revs should always be kept high. In other words, the horse must not lose impulsion or rhythm during the slowing-up period, and if he should do so, the rider must quickly restore both in time for the fence. It is worth studying human athletes during a steeplechase. Note how they shorten their stride prior to each obstacle so that they can easily find a take-off point. This is when they re-balance and gather their energy for the jump. They lose no time or momentum whilst 'setting-up'. We must use the same principles when preparing our horses for each fence.

This transfer of the horse's balance and gathering of impulsion/energy is executed by the rider moving from forward position to a more upright position with the seat lowered into the saddle a minimum of six strides away so that it is in a strong driving position if needed. Having his shoulders further back helps the rider to keep in behind his horse until take-off. During these last few strides, the rider can feel if the horse is losing power or rhythm and can counteract it before it is too late. If the rider stays in forward position, he will have less chance to get in behind his horse to avert a problem – there will be no time to alter from a forward seat to a defensive seat if the horse suddenly changes his forward-going attitude. Various types of fence – such as big ditches or fences with roofs over – may appear menacing to a horse, so the rider must be prepared for any adverse effect.

At all times the rider must think 'forward movement' (forward does *not* mean fast) and balance and rhythm. He should then wait for the fence and not throw the horse onto his forehand in the last couple of strides (watch the human athlete – he only has two legs to worry about and no weight on his back). With difficult fences such as coffins, fences into water or other spooky obstacles, it is important that the horse has plenty of impulsion and is on a bouncy, shorter stride (*not* bouncing up and down on the spot with the rider 'looking for a stride'). This will offer less chance of the rider 'going for a long one' – a horse will be tempted to put down again if asked to jump off a long stride at a fence of this nature. This is a recipe for disaster. The rider must create a bouncy canter and maintain it until the horse takes off.

Jumping fences on the angle is acceptable provided that the angle is not too sharp, so inviting a run-out, that the horse is trained to jump angle fences and that the fence is not a drop fence. Never jump a drop on the angle because if the horse drops a leg (and angled jumps do invite a horse to do this) it will have the effect of spinning him sideways with little chance of recovery if the landing is lower.

Cross-country riding demands attack and a positive attitude. Any negative thoughts or lack of confidence will inevitably lead to a problem. Even if you are anxious about a fence, imagine yourself sailing over it and you will. If you anticipate trouble, it will be there to greet you!

44. The start. Here is an eager, controlled horse leaving the start-box, confident of his job. You can see that he knows where he is going and what he is setting out to do. There is no question of him weaving and wandering to the first fence. He and his rider are committed and concentrating on the job ahead. It is important that you set off with a positive attitude. If you meander out of the start-box, with your horse half asleep, it is asking for trouble. On the other hand, you do not want to wind your horse up into an excitable frenzy so that you make him neurotic and upset. Experience with riding and understanding different horses will help you to find the balance between making your horse 'on the ball' and making him tense and worried. Alas, rider nerves often transfer themselves to the horse, and many times an excitable, plunging horse at the start is the result of a nervous, anxious rider. A determined rider will instil grit and attack – a nervous rider will make his horse nervous.

45. The first fence. Although the smallest obstacle on the course, it should not be dismissed. A variety of factors make it a fence to be respected. The horse is going away from home and his friends and into the unknown. He will probably set off – particularly a young horse who has no idea what is to come – with a certain amount of reluctance and will trace a wandering line to the first fence. He may then spook and even stop. If riding a youngster, the rider must be aware of this sort of reaction over the first few fences. An older horse may take a totally different approach. He may set off very eager and totally ignore the fence, almost tripping over it. Experience will tell you how your horse will react.

The first few fences are usually straightforward, then you come to the more demanding ones which require athletic ability. If you allow the horse to flatten and hurdle the early fences, it will come as rather a shock when he is suddenly asked to shorten for a tricky one. It is a mistake to 'hurdle' any fence, but a straightforward fence such as a brush fence will allow the horse to arrive with a minimum amount of setting up. He should still not jump it off his forehand. Every fence should be jumped with balance and rhythm, however small or simple. It should then become second nature for horse and rider to set themselves up for every fence, the necessary amount depending on the severity of the particular fence.

46. Jumping an upright. Although the rider is allowing the horse the necessary freedom with her hands, her shoulders are exaggeratedly low, which would necessitate excess body movement between elements if this were part of a combination.

Jumping an upright cross-country fence is the same as jumping an upright show-jump except that the pace will be quicker. The essence is still balance and rhythm and from a galloping approach it will be necessary for the rider to re-balance the horse and transfer the weight from the forehand to the hindquarters. In between fences the rider takes forward position to stay in balance. The faster a horse goes, the further forward his centre of gravity will be. The weight must be redistributed to bring the centre of gravity back before a fence and, depending upon the nature of the obstacle, this transfer of balance may vary. An upright fence demands accuracy, for the choice of take-off points is limited due to the lack of ground-line. There is nothing to back off the horse, therefore he must be able to lengthen or shorten his stride with ease. He must have rhythm, and in order to have rhythm he must be going forward in balance. From the forward galloping position, the rider must draw his shoulder back and sit up more, making connection with the saddle by sitting lightly, then close the hand, keeping the leg closed too to make sure that the horse does not lose forward movement. The operation should be similar to slowing down a car by using the gears rather than the brakes. If the brakes are used without any gear change, the engine will labour and the car will lose power and the ability to quicken. The same happens if the rider slows the horse down by just using his hand – the pace will slow, but the horse will also stop going forward and so lose balance, rhythm and impulsion. It is of paramount importance to maintain these when jumping any fence, and all the more important if this fence is sited on undulating terrain. It should be second nature to sit correctly over every fence, however straightforward. In this way, the rider will not be caught out if the horse makes a mistake one day.

47. Spread. A lovely picture of balance and harmony over a big fence. Note the straight line from stirrup (the foot is home – a good idea for cross-country riding), through knee, elbow, shoulder and ear, and also the straight line from horse's mouth through rein to hand.

Spread fences on the cross-country may be either square oxers, such as in this photo, or ascending spreads, e.g. steeplechase fences, triple bars, sharks teeth and elephant traps. Ascending spreads are the easiest fences to jump whether in the show-jumping ring or on a cross-country course. They offer the greatest range of take-off points and prevent the horse from getting too close at the highest point, so putting less premium on foreleg technique. An ascending spread is inviting to jump and, although an adjustment of balance will be necessary, there is not so great a need for a big weight transferral as there is for a square parallel. A square parallel may either be constructed from poles, or may be hidden as a table, hay rack or footbridge. Any parallel puts a premium on balance, rhythm and impulsion – a parallel can be thought of as an upright spread. It requires the same accuracy as an upright but demands scope as well. The spread gives the fence a more imposing look and there is more for the horse to respect and look at. Provided that the rider re-balances the horse and concentrates on having sufficient impulsion for the size of the fence, the horse should jump spread fences out of his rhythm without problems.

Table fences have in the past caused a high proportion of falls. As riders, we see the fence as imposing and solid and we know it is a spread. The horse sees a table much in the same way as he sees a sleeper wall. There is little for him to judge on where to take off. Many novice riders see tables as straightforward, inviting fences. They seem to be the sorts of fences which encourage these novice riders to send their horses on long strides on the old 'one, two, three' method. All too often, the horse, having been put on his forehand, tries to put in an extra stride with the inevitable result.

A square parallel is unforgiving and demands balance, impulsion and rhythm – any lack of these and the horse will pay the penalty. If the fence is sited downhill or on uneven ground, the rider must ensure that the rhythm and balance are not lost and that the horse keeps coming forward. Probably the most difficult feeling to learn is how to balance a horse without losing forward movement. This only comes from practice and experience, coupled with an understanding of what is necessary.

48. Step up. Two horses jumping the same steps up. The chestnut horse is jumping in good balance and can easily be imagined popping up subsequent steps with no problems. The rider's position is very good. It presents a picture of balance, control and harmony. The bay horse shows a different sight. The horse has taken off further away and has made a much flatter jump. He is on his forehand and looks as if the next step up might well cause problems. The steps are small, so the combination may get away with making a mistake. The first horse and rider would be able to jump any size step whereas the second pair are struggling to clear this small one. It is important to arrive at steps in a short, bouncy canter to avoid 'belly-flopping' onto them like this second horse. These two pictures present a clear message and are worth studying.

49. Step up. An interesting angle – you can see clearly how important it is for the horse to have his front feet far enough onto the step for there to be room for the back feet to land. If the horse lacks impulsion and only just makes the step or bank, he will scrabble with his hind feet and have an uncomfortable moment. The rider has slipped his reins to allow the horse to use his neck and is sitting in good central balance. If his shoulders were further forward, it would put too much weight on the horse's forehand.

Steps and banks are a test of a horse's power and athletic ability. The horse must jump off his hocks, so he must be light on the forehand on the approach. This means that he must be re-balanced to a great degree if the fence has been preceded by a long gallop. The approach should be a short, bouncy canter full of impulsion with balance and rhythm, enabling the horse to spring up the steps with agility. With a series of steps, the rider must keep his weight forward, maintain the impulsion and not sit complacently after jumping one step.

50. Bank. This horse looks as if he arrived too fast at this bank. As a result, he has not had time to get his undercarriage out. The rider is sitting well, giving the horse all possible assistance to recover. If the rider were sitting too far forward, all the weight would be on the horse's forehand and he would be unable to find his feet. By keeping the weight on the hindquarters, the forehand is free to rise up – a horse always gets up front end first.

51. Drop. A drop fence perfectly executed. Balance here is vital. The rider's body has a great influence on the horse's balance and from these photos you can imagine how a horse could easily be made to fall on landing if the rider's weight were too far forward. On the approach, the horse must be well balanced; if the horse is unbalanced at take-off, he will undoubtedly be unbalanced on landing. It is important never to arrive at a drop too fast, on an accelerating pace or on the angle. An even pace is important. If the horse slows down to a drop, the jump will be an 'up and down' jump and the drop will be more apparent. An even pace and rhythm will help to keep maximum balance and the rider must be ready to brace against the stirrup and keep the shoulders back and head up to help his horse to the full – don't forget to slip the reins!

Note the rider's perfect position throughout. The seat is low, the heels down, lower leg forward ready to brace for the drop, the reins slipped and the horse allowed freedom, but a contact remaining so that the rider can 'pick up' the horse if necessary should he peck on landing. A loose rein would give no help at all. The rider's arm is low and relaxed and the shoulders back with the head up. An example for anyone.

This is a major drop fence – a lesser drop would not appear as dramatic because the angle of the horse would not be so great.

Always take note of the landings of fences when walking a course. It is one thing for the horse to be taken by surprise – he will not know there is a drop – but you want to be able to be prepared. An innocent, inviting hedge changes character if there is a big drop on the other side.

52. Drop. This is not a good position to be in! In fact it is dangerous. The lack of security of the lower leg has allowed the body to flop forward and the rider is totally reliant upon the horse's neck for support. The bigger the drop, the more emphasis is placed on the rider's security of seat and correct position.

53. Dell. This is a variation of a sunken road with a fence on the top of a hill, another in the bottom of a dip, followed by another element at the top of the rise out of the dell.

The fence going into this dell is obviously difficult and the horse is jumping it stickily – no doubt he sees the fence in the bottom. The rider has a good position over the first element with a correct safety seat. However, she is then slow to regain her position (note the long rein) and so be able to keep her horse in balance and with impulsion and rhythm. The horse, on his forehand, is unable and unwilling to take off and a problem has resulted. Speed of recovery after an anxious moment is crucial when there are subsequent elements involved.

54. Bounce. This horse has jumped in boldly and is bouncing the second element. A bounce fence demands an agile and athletic horse. The horse has to jump two or possibly three elements without taking a stride in between. The distance between elements may vary depending on the siting, but 10–14 feet would be average.

The shorter the distance, the more controlled and bouncy the pace of approach must be and the more athletic the horse in his jumping. It is important that the horse is prepared correctly and is not allowed to arrive at the bounce long and flat. He must be on his hocks, with impulsion, balance and rhythm so that he can literally bounce through the combination. The rider must keep a contact throughout to help the horse take off again as soon as he has landed. The body movement should be minimised to help keep balance and to avoid putting too much weight on the horse's shoulders on landing. The forward swing should be as little as possible. Wait until the horse takes off, and allow the jump to bend your hips (see Diagram 11).

55. This horse has landed short over the first element and has put in a short stride. Fortunately, the rider has kept behind the horse and the fence is safely negotiated. Had the rider thrown his weight forward and so unbalanced the horse, it might have proved disastrous.

56. Trakehner. The bold horse (*above*) is jumping over the log without worrying about the ditch in the least. His ears are pricked and he is jumping it beautifully. The rider is in a good position, made easier by her horse's attitude – a picture of harmony and balance. The other combination shows a different picture. The horse appears to have been reluctant to jump and has done so with less fluency, giving his rider an anxious moment. The rider is in a precarious position. It is always much easier to look stylish on a horse who is jumping smoothly. One which does not jump boldly is difficult to sit on well, causing the rider to take evasive action and possibly overdoing it as this rider is.

57. Water. This horse has obviously jumped boldly into the water. Water has an unbalancing effect and can stop the forward movement very quickly. The rider must therefore keep his weight back to avoid overloading the front end and causing a fall.

This rider has his weight firmly in his heels and the lower leg is ready to brace against any possible impact. The seat is low, the shoulders back and the head up. He has slipped his reins in readiness for the drop into the water and the horse is on a light contact – an excellent example.

Horses have a natural fear of water and must have implicit faith in their riders. Confidence is gained slowly from experience. Some horses are naturally less timid than others when first introduced to water. Trust takes time to build up but can quickly be destroyed if the horse has a fright at a water fence. It is up to the rider to minimise this risk by always presenting his horse correctly at any water fence. The unbalancing effect of water means that the horse must be in perfect balance before jumping into it. The rider must re-balance in plenty of time so that the horse is prepared well in advance and has time to assess what he has to do. The horse *must* maintain forward movement at this stage, otherwise it will be difficult to recreate impulsion in time for the fence.

The horse should arrive in a bouncy canter, full of impulsion (to counteract any hesitation). The rider must ride strongly, without allowing the horse to get long, and must stay in behind the horse with his shoulders back until the horse takes off. When he swings forward, he should keep more upright than with a plain fence so that he is ready to sit up as he lands – note the upright position of this rider.

If the approach is too fast or the jump very bold, the horse is more likely to lose his balance on landing in the water. Once in the water, the rider should quickly pick up the rhythm of whatever pace the horse has landed in. If the rider tries to change pace, the horse will lose valuable impulsion and balance. If there is a fence in the water, the rider must work hard to keep rhythm, balance and impulsion and at the same time keep the contact. The horse must be between hand and leg. The rider should sit up and keep his body still to help the balance. It requires a great amount of effort to jump out of water, so the rider must be positive without interfering with the horse's stride or balance. Try to avoid 'going for a stride' in water. Keep the rhythm, keep riding forward and allow the horse to jump the fences.

58. Two examples of landing and turning after a drop into water (*left*). In the first one the rider is sitting well. She has the weight in her heel, her shoulders back and her head up. She has slipped the reins, but is still guiding the horse round to the left. The picture below shows a rider too far forward and in front of the balance. If the horse should peck badly she appears to be in no position to help him recover and may indeed force him to fall or fall off herself. She is, however, looking up and guiding the horse in the necessary direction. If her shoulders were further back, and therefore her balance further back, it would be a good picture.

In going through water, the horse must be prevented from falling onto his forehand. This is a good picture of a rider in behind his horse, with a secure leg, driving his horse forward towards a fence out of water. Although he has slipped the reins, he has maintained a contact and the horse is going forward, well prepared for the fence ahead. Key points: heels down, head up and shoulders behind the movement.

59. When assessing the difficulty of a water fence, the attention is drawn to the fence into the water or a fence in the water itself. What is commonly ignored is the innocent-looking step out of the water, which may be on its own or connected to another fence immediately afterwards. Steps out of water are always difficult to jump and a horse has difficulty judging when to take off. Splashing water and the drag of the water are the contributing factors. The rider's best way to help is to keep riding forward, keeping the horse balanced and between hand and leg and concentrating on keeping as good a rhythm as possible. The horse must decide when to take off and the rider has to be ready to stay in balance and not get left behind if the horse takes off at an unexpected moment. If the rider is left behind, he must slip the reins to avoid yanking the horse in the mouth. This is all the more important if there is another fence following on a related distance – the rider must try to catch up with the horse to enable him to jump subsequent elements. See here how the horse uses his head and neck as he comes up the step out of the water. The rider is allowing maximum freedom and is sitting well in balance. You can imagine how the horse would be hindered should the rider lose his balance and so restrict the horse.

Quick reactions are vital – these only come from experience. A correct position means that there is minimum loss of balance, whereas an unbalanced position will aggravate the situation considerably. Quick reactions are an essential part of eventing, giving the rider the ability to recover from mistakes and so avoid penalty. Slow reactions will lead to trouble and the inability to recover from even a slight error.

60. Arrowheads require precise riding. The horse must be balanced and absolutely straight. A fence like this (or angles or corners, for example) allows no room for error. Everything must be just right for a successful jump. A young horse should not be presented with such fences until his training has made him completely obedient otherwise he may learn how easy it is to run out and may try to perfect the technique of this naughty habit. The horse must know exactly where he is expected to jump when presented with a vary narrow fence. The rider must have the horse absolutely between hand and leg and he must stay well in behind the horse until he actually takes off. One split second in front of the movement gives the horse the opportunity to run out. This rider is in a perfect position, slightly behind his horse and ready to adopt the driving seat for a subsequent element. Note the head up, the low seat and security of the lower leg.

61. Ditches and coffins. This shows a good position over a ditch, with secure leg and head up, looking in the direction of the next fence. The horse is hanging slightly left, but the rider has him in control ready to straighten up for the next element.

The photo on the right shows an unbalanced horse who has not jumped the ditch cleanly. If the next element were close and of a demanding nature, it is questionable whether this combination would be able to recover in time to jump it. The horse must have been unable to adjust his stride to meet the ditch at a suitable take-off point, which suggests a lack of rhythm on the approach. (Remember: forward movement + balance = rhythm = ability to lengthen or shorten the stride.)

A coffin – which will include one or two ditches on either flat or unlevel terrain – is one of the most influential fences on a cross-country course. Most courses have coffins and, since they cause so much trouble, it is worth schooling over a variety before attempting to jump one in competition. Confidence is all-important. The horse must understand that although the distances are short, he is in no danger of jumping straight into the ditch – a possibility if the approach is too fast and unbalanced. The same bouncy canter as for a sunken road or water jump should be maintained, with the hocks well-engaged and the forehand light. The revs should be high but the pace controlled. The horse must use himself athletically and not jump with a flat parabola. A coffin may be spooky and catch a horse unawares.

The rider must be prepared for this and maintain forward movement even if the horse hesitates. The rider's body must stay behind the horse s movement to keep the horse in front of him. The forward swing should be minimal to reduce body movement through the coffin and help stabilise the balance. As soon as the horse has landed over one element, the rider should be in position ready for the next one. Speed of reaction is essential with any tricky fence and being ready for your horse's reaction only comes with practice and experience. A novice rider will find that the horse has already run out or stopped before he notices that something is amiss. An experienced rider will pick up any vibes and anticipate his horse's reaction to a variety of fences.

62. Road crossing. Although this horse has negotiated both elements without fault, the general impression is rather lacking in control. It is not a neat display, taking the minimum out of the horse. It looks as if the line taken was not straight, and in fact the rider can be seen trying to correct her horse over the first element. She has a loose, flapping rein over the second element which indicates that the horse is not 'between hand and leg' as he should be. The rider's stirrups look rather too long, which is not helping the security of her seat.

These two photos show the final element of the road crossing. The one above provides an example of perfect rider position – low seat, security of lower leg, head up, shoulders not too low and hand allowing freedom as necessary. The other horse is showing a good, neat jump with excellent foreleg technique, which is spoilt by the poor rider position. He has no security at all in the seat and his weight is in front of his horse.

63. Sunken road. A good example of correct (shoulders back, security of lower leg, hands down, head up, reins slipped) position. The agility and balance required for jumping a sunken road is influenced by the rider's position. The horse must approach in a bouncy canter, full of impulsion with the all-important rhythm and balance. This rhythm and balance must be maintained throughout and the rider must keep a good position to ensure this. Luckington Lane at Badminton is a major test of rider position and balance as well as horse agility.

64. Corners. A corner fence requires precise riding and allows no room for error. Any misjudgement will result in a run-out, a fall or just a bad experience which may affect the confidence of horse and rider. The approach and line to the fence are all-important. It must be at the correct pace with balance and rhythm, with the line of approach at right-angles to an imaginary line dissecting the angle. The closeness to the point of the corner depends on its width. It is useful to line up with a landmark when walking the course to help find the correct line to any difficult fence where the line of approach is vital. Beware of corners on the edge of woods or trees. The darkness is a distraction and will encourage horses to drift away from it. Accurate riding and an honest, well-trained horse which jumps straight are essential.

This series of photos shows a horse drifting to the left and to possible trouble. The rider has done an excellent job in averting a disaster. Her balance is good, with the weight in the heel and, as a result, she is able to steer the horse in mid-air. Had her bodyweight been collapsed over the horse's neck, she would not have been in a position to help. With the weight on his forehand, the horse would not have been able to turn in the air. Here is another example of good position preserving the balance and allowing the effective riding which is necessary in an awkward moment.

65. This is a **fence at the top of a hill**. The rider is in the defensive position with his body and has stayed in behind his horse on take-off. He has slipped the reins to allow the horse freedom. His head is up and he has good security in the lower leg. If the horse should peck, the rider would be in a good position to help him recover his balance.

When walking the course, notice the impression a fence on the top of a hill gives you, particularly as you approach it for the first time. It will appear as if you are going to jump into space. It is only as you get nearer that you realise that there is somewhere to land, and from close up the fence looks innocent and very small. Remember that the horse will only get your first impression as he approaches at speed. He will have no time to notice that there is somewhere to land, so must have total obedience and faith in his rider. He may well hesitate, so the rider must be in behind his horse to combat this as well as have created sufficient impulsion for the horse to keep going forward even if he hesitates slightly. If you only have just enough impulsion for a tricky fence, a hesitation will metaphorically 'empty the tank of petrol' and you will give the horse a chance to refuse. Feel that you have changed into high revs with the engine roaring, ready to go – think balance, impulsion and rhythm with a positive attitude and keep your horse in front of you at all times. The moment the rider commits his body before his horse, the horse can draw back underneath him and stop. Wait until the horse takes off, even if you feel slightly left behind. There are times when it is better to be left behind – you can always slip your reins to avoid catching the horse's mouth. The downhill landing has caught this horse (*above*) by surprise and he has tipped the top. An insecure seat and lower leg have nearly been the downfall of this rider (she did recover!). Imagine a perfect position superimposed on this mistake and you can see how important a good, secure seat and lower leg are in moments of crisis.

66. Uphill and downhill fences. When riding up and down hills, the rider's position should remain in relation to gravity. When riding uphill, the rider's body should incline forward so that the balance is with the horse's movement. When riding downhill, the shoulders are drawn back a little, with the lower leg taking the weight and giving security. If you lean too far back, you are behind the balance and will be left behind if the horse has to jump a fence on this incline. Fences sited uphill and downhill are good tests of horse and rider balance. When going uphill, a horse automatically has his hocks underneath him, therefore uphill fences tend to jump well. Downhill, the horse's weight will fall onto his forehand and the forward motion increases this. To jump a fence downhill, the horse has to prop with his forelegs to keep the weight on his hindquarters. A steep downhill approach to a fence will have the effect of shortening a horse's stride, whereas if the incline is gentle, it will encourage the stride to lengthen. This must be borne in mind when studying a combination built on a hill. It is difficult to predict what effect each individual incline will have, so it is useful to be able to watch a number of horses jump through the combination so that you can see how they cope with the ups or downs.

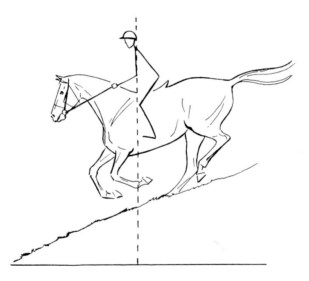

This is where cross-country riding differs from show-jumping. In a show-jumping ring, the terrain is more or less flat and the horse's stride can be predicted accurately. With the ups and downs of cross-country, it is impossible always to gauge the length of stride a horse will take. A rider cannot dominate the stride pattern to the same extent as he can in show-jumping. This is why it is so important that the horse learns to look for himself and to look after himself to a greater degree when jumping. If the horse totally relies on his rider to find his take-off stride, he will find jumping off unlevel terrain rather confusing. Riders often panic when faced with an uphill fence. Because they can imagine the effort it would require for them to jump it themselves, they think the horse will struggle. This is a time when the horse's four legs are a definite advantage! The power generated from the hocks should not be underestimated – all the rider has to do is to keep the impulsion, balance and rhythm, and the horse will ping over any uphill fence with ease.

When riding a downhill fence, it is of paramount importance that the rider does not in any way alter the balance, but allows the horse to balance himself by propping slightly. He should just keep the leg on and wait for the fence, ensuring that the horse keeps the rhythm and that he keeps the balance. The rider who fires his horse into his fences will be in big trouble with a downhill fence unless he learns to sit still. He may get away with incorrect riding over small fences but his Waterloo will come when the fences get bigger. If you always try to ride small fences correctly – and being small, you can concentrate on everything being right because you have no worries over a tiny fence – you will automatically ride correctly over bigger, more demanding obstacles when it really does matter that you do nothing wrong.

67. This horse is **fighting** for his head on the approach to a fence. In the first frame, the rider's leg is further forward than is effective and he appears to be trying to steady the horse with his hand alone. As a result, the horse's hocks are not engaged, he is not balanced, so he is resisting. In the second frame, the rider has relaxed his hands, his legs are in a better position and the horse has relaxed too and is in a good shape to jump the fence.

68. Two horses **twisting** over their fences. The first horse is jumping a trakehner, and the rider is sitting central and has kept her balance, allowing the horse freedom to find his own. The other photo depicts an uncomfortable picture for horse and rider. It looks as though the rider is riding too long to be able to take advantage of bracing against the stirrup in anxious moments such as these. It is important that the saddle allows you to ride short enough so that you can use the stirrup for security of the lower leg.

69. Refusing. Alas, the rider has gone first and, when the horse stopped, she didn't. Here is proof of the necessity to stay behind your horse, with a secure lower leg with grip, until he takes off. This is a luckier escape than a situation in which the horse tries to put in a short stride and fails, somersaulting over the fence. Wait for the fence to come to you and allow the horse to take off before you commit yourself and this picture will not be you! When riding cross-country, you must keep the horse in front of you at all times and always be prepared for the unexpected. Your position should scarcely alter in moments of crisis. This is what separates the average rider from the good one. The ability to anticipate and have a good, secure position and balance comes from experience and hard work.

70. Here is a straightforward, **innocent-looking** fence which has caused real problems. The horse has not respected the timber wagon. This would be one of the most insignificant-looking obstacles on the course. As a result, the horse has not taken much notice of it and the rider has failed in his efforts to set up the horse sufficiently. Perhaps he has forgotten to take sufficient account of the fact that the horse will have little to 'look at' and will therefore need more re-balancing and preparing than for a huge, yawning trakehner, for example. Always beware of fences which offer little for the horse to look at. The less there is to back off the horse, the more important it is for the rider to set him up and help him. First and last fences tend to fall into this category. Being straightforward, the rider does not worry about them unduly and with the horse's mind probably half on something else (especially either going away from or towards home), a lack of concentration may result in a mistake. Remember, you have not finished until you have crossed the finishing line. There is a chance the horse may be getting a little weary and therefore long in his outline and stride (a tired horse will find it more difficult to bring his hocks underneath him to find balance and impulsion). The last fence means you are so near yet possibly so far from your goal of a fast, clear round. Ensure that you still balance the horse and jump the last correctly before keeping the horse between hand and leg and riding him to the finish.

Conclusion

There is no substitute for experience in any sport. To benefit from experience means that you are capable of learning from your mistakes. Everyone makes mistakes; every horse makes mistakes. The way to improve and avoid making the *same* mistakes is by analysing what went wrong and why and how you are going to avoid it happening again. If we repeatedly make the same mistake, we are not allowing ourselves to learn from experience. Instead of confidence gradually building up, it will start to ebb and we will make more mistakes. Once we learn from our experiences, we should become effective, confident riders capable of riding at a certain level. A very good rider will learn from his experiences and, coupled with natural talent, hard work and a suitable horse, will be successful.

It is often said: 'Oh, she's a hopeless competitor.' What makes a good competitor? It is a determination and will to succeed coupled with an ability to ride to the best of one's capabilities under pressure. Probably the most important aspect is confidence in yourself and your horse. Confidence can only be built up through training and consequently the knowledge that you can do it. Confidence comes across as a cool, calm and collected attitude with no outward signs of nerves or tension. Confidence is easily destroyed in some people and horses. These types must be constantly bolstered to ensure that their confidence remains buoyant. Different people require different methods to ensure that their confidence remains high. It may mean jumping only small fences at home or it may mean jumping bigger fences to let you know that your horse can easily do so.

As a teacher, it is important to understand your pupils' mentalities and to be able to help them with their confidence and that of their horses. Even the most tense rider can improve his or her attitude by thorough training at home. By repetition, it will slowly become ingrained in the rider how to cope with becoming stiff and tense. The more thorough and correct the training and work at home, the more chance there will be of everything not going to pieces in competition. If the work at home is moderate, it will only be worse in public!

Good horses make good riders. Not many people are fortunate enough always to have good horses to ride. Most of us have to make do with an average animal and try to make it into a better one. The very good rider is able to convert a moderate horse into a good one by training and schooling. The less talented rider will need a good horse to help him. Training an 'ordinary' horse to become something special is satisfying indeed. Anyone can ride a good horse – the challenge is trying to make an average one good. In order to train a horse, it is vital to understand exactly what you are trying to achieve and at what stage. Ultimately, you are aiming for an obedient horse who can carry out all your commands without resistance. This takes time – for the horse to learn the aids, to strengthen and become supple enough to carry out the necessary movements on the flat which will then enable him to jump well. The horse's training goes through stages and levels of performance and he should not be expected to perform beyond his level of training.

The most important aspect of learning is understanding – whether it be horse or rider. Until you and your horse understand what is being asked of you, you will never improve. As a rider, once you have truly understood the principles of rhythm and balance and learnt to feel forward movement, your learning curve will be steep. A talented rider may quickly grasp the feeling of rhythm, balance and forward movement, whereas a less talented, tense rider may take longer. As a rider, it is often difficult to feel what you are doing. Video cameras are invaluable in helping to underline what a rider is doing if he cannot feel it himself. Invariably it comes as a shock to the rider when he sees that in fact his heels are not down, or that his shoulders are stooped, for example. What you think you are doing and what you are actually doing can be very different. The camera will clarify everything!

Whatever the sport, whether it be golf, tennis or riding, it is imperative that the technique is correct. Badly timed balls will not find their goal; similarly, lack of balance and rhythm will have dire results.

So what is it that makes someone such as Mark Todd such a brilliant all-round horseman? It is a combination of a correct seat with balance and security, an ability to keep his horse in rhythm and balance and keep it coming forward at the same time. He has an accurate eye and his experience in riding a multitude of different horses in different spheres of competition – show-jumping, racing and eventing – gives him a vast experience from which to learn and benefit. Finally, he instils confidence into his horses by being confident himself – confident that he is asking the horse to do the correct thing and that his horse is capable of doing it. Watch and study the top riders – see how still they sit, how they keep the rhythm and keep riding forward with the horse in balance beneath them. Try to imagine you are the same when you ride – imagine you look the same as you approach a fence and jump it. Although you need to 'be yourself' it does not matter if you allow yourself to be influenced by good riders. Learning is imitation to a certain extent – imitation is free! Every top rider has his or her idols on whom they have styled themselves even if it is only sub-consciously. Study riders and study them with critical appreciation – understand what they are doing when they make it look so easy.

At all times when you are riding, you should look neat and tidy, whatever your shape. The moment you lose balance, you cease to be neat. Imagine Ginny Elliot, Mark Todd, John Whitaker, Richard Dunwoody – they are all neat and tidy. Look at their photographs, then look at the less experienced riders and see how they vary – in many cases they appear untidy. When you get photos sent to you from events, look at them and compare them with those of top riders. Decide where you are going wrong and make every effort to improve yourself. And it does require effort too!

Keep the all-important words in your mind as you ride any fence: forward movement (keep your arms light and relaxed), balance (keep the horse straight and between hand and leg) and rhythm, and maintain this all the way to the fence (let the fence come to you). Remember, the worst crime is to get in front of your horse, so forget the old Pony Club adage of 'throw your heart over and the pony will follow' – it does not work! Keep the horse in front of you – in the hand and in front of the leg, and then keep your body still. You are riding a real horse, not a rocking horse – many people seem to forget that . . .

Jumping is simple. We, the riders, make it complicated and bring difficulties on ourselves and our horses. If only we could allow ourselves to ride more naturally and give our horses the chance to concentrate on the fences to be jumped. If only we could sit still and just allow the horse to arrive, undisturbed but with enough impulsion to jump, at each fence. If only we could reproduce more for the horse the feeling that he can carry our weight with ease and be able to balance and re-balance himself as necessary. If only we did not interfere to the detriment of the basic requirements to jump any fence – rhythm, balance and impulsion

– then jumping would be easy. Where the hard work comes in is training the horse to be able to carry his weight and that of his rider on his hocks so that he can balance himself without having to rely on his rider's hand. This is where correct flat work is vital – not 'dressage' with the horse forced into a restricted shape, but suppleness and balance and the ability to keep a rhythm at all times.

Once we have established that with our horses, then jumping is uncomplicated whatever the pace. The principles are all the same. Where we must not go wrong is to confuse not interfering with being totally passive. It is often hard work requiring maximum effort to ensure that the horse does keep coming forward with impulsion and that he does not lose rhythm or balance, but this effort must be used correctly and not detrimentally. We come back to experience – it is only by repetition that we learn how to balance a tired horse and to decide at what pace we should approach various fences.

Learn, understand, experience, learn from it and try again (repetition). Finally, do not despair. Provided that you are not genuinely frightened of riding, you can overcome any slight anxieties about jumping as long as you understand what you should be doing and why. It then all makes sense, and you should be able to take advantage of your superior wits rather than indulging in a physical struggle. A few stone versus half a ton is no contest – but, brains for brains, we should come out on top!

Index

Note: balance, rhythm and good position appear throughout the book too often to be noted in the index except for their definitions.